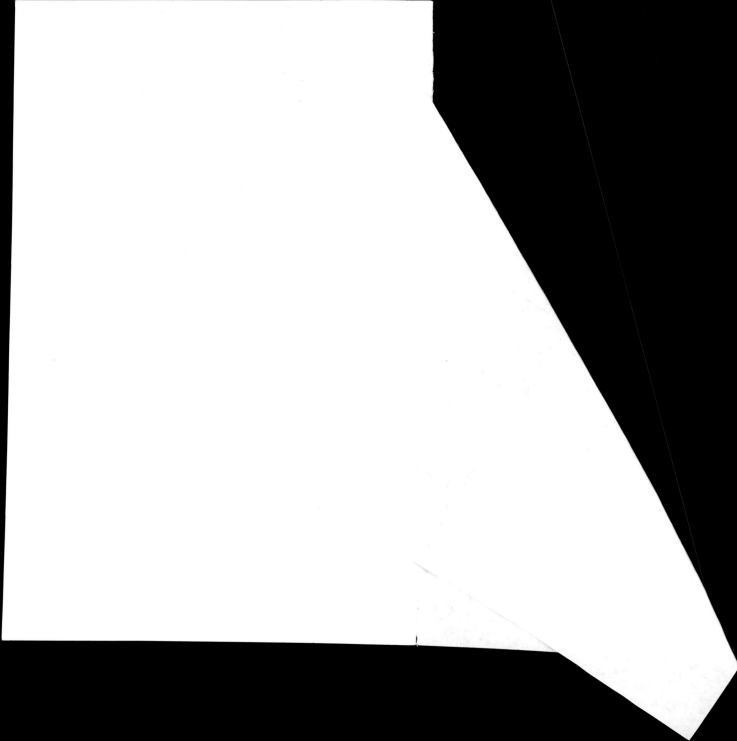

STEP BY STEP

31 DAYS TO A DEEPER WALK WITH GOD

Gregg Harris

P.O. Box 1
La Mirada, CA 90637-0001
1-800-523-3480
FEBC.org

Published by Dunham Books
Copyright © 2007 by Gregg Harris and
FEBC
Published 2007

ISBN: 978-1-934590-22-5

All Scripture quotations, unless otherwise indicated,
are taken from the New International Version.

Printed in the United States of America

For more information, please contact:
Dunham Books
15455 Dallas Parkway, Sixth Floor
Addison, TX 75001
972-764-3516
dunhambooks.com

STEP BY STEP

Foreword

Gregg Harris is at the vanguard of 21st century leaders of Christian ministries. As President of Far East Broadcasting Company (FEBC), Harris helms a worldwide media ministry that delivers the gospel message to the literal far corners of our planet. As you hold this book in your hands, Christian radio programs in indigenous languages are being broadcast to millions, even billions, of people in the earth's eastern hemisphere. That's what FEBC does 24 hours a day and Gregg Harris is the man God has set apart to lead that effort.

In *Step by Step*, Gregg reminds us of some of the foundational truths that are so crucial and life-changing. In this book, Gregg focuses on the relevancy of Scripture in each of our lives, no matter what our native tongue may be. He weaves in pertinent illustrations, excellent insights, and occasionally, even real-life FEBC stories. Each of his thirty-one chapters is a Bible lesson in itself.

Indeed, I enjoyed using *Step by Step* as a daily devotional book for an entire month.

You'll find *Step by Step* thought-provoking and uplifting. While its truths are timeless, the relevancy and urgency of each of these Bible certainties is manna for the next generation. Gregg is absolutely on target!

I know Gregg Harris to be a man of vision and utter dedication to bringing the truth of God's Word to a hurting world. He does it every day in his leadership of FEBC. And he does it in the book you're about to read.

May you be blessed by its wisdom and may God bring a rich harvest of souls through His anointed Word.

Just remember, as you are turning the pages of this book, these same timeless truths are being broadcast in teeming cities, crowded prisons, jungle huts and secret churches from Saipan to Moscow, Korea to Calcutta.

And lives are being changed… *Step by Step*.

Don Piper
October 2007
Author of *90 Minutes in Heaven: A True Story of Death and Life*

Introduction

The challenge facing every generation of Christ followers is to understand and learn to respond to the spirit of their age. Like the men of Issachar, "who understood the times and knew what Israel should do" (1 Chronicles 12:32), you and I must comprehend the realities of our world *and* be able to respond according to God's eternal truth.

We may not like the world we live in (as a matter of fact, we're not supposed to), but we are to engage our world as part of God's redemptive plan. Isolation is not an option for those who call Christ, "Lord." That's why Jesus, in John 17, prayed this prayer for His disciples… and for you and me…, "they are not of the world, any more than I am of the world. My prayer is not that You take them out of the world, but that You protect them from the evil one."

The world you and I are called to live in today is characterized by two dominant themes: relativism and complexity. We live at a time when everything is considered relative. The idea of absolute truth is considered heresy in our day and age. "Believe what you want, but don't force it on me" is the mantra of our age. "Whatever works for you is fine, but don't try to tell me how to live my life." I do find it amusing, though, that the only thing people are not "allowed" to believe in is the concept of absolute truth. It's a strange thing for relativists to be so dogmatic!

How then should we respond to relativism? First, by not confusing relativism with freedom of conscience.

Throughout history, Christians have supported freedom of conscience. But there is a fundamental difference between relativism and freedom of conscience. Relativism says there are no absolutes, so each person must define truth for himself. Freedom of conscience says that every human being is created in the image of God and, as such, has the capacity to exercise their will in choosing their beliefs.

Freedom of conscience does not abandon the concept of absolute truth; rather, it upholds it by emphasizing that each individual can choose to accept or reject truth based on the freedom God has given them.

But we not only live in a relativistic age, we live in a time of staggering complexity. Technology has improved our lives in many ways, yet it has also introduced exponential increases in the intricacy and speed of our lives. As I write these words, I am sitting in a hotel room in the Philippines. Having just arrived from the U.S. a few hours ago, I called my wife and daughter on my mobile phone. What a great blessing to be able to stay in touch so easily when I'm 7000 miles away from home. But that same phone sometimes seems to be like an electronic leash, which intrudes on my life and demands a response at inconvenient times.

And those possibilities for instantaneous communication seem to only increase each year as new wireless data and voice options come to market. But it's that ability to communicate instantaneously that often creates increasing stress and expectations for us to do more in less time.

Today we are able to communicate, travel, be entertained, and receive and manage information in ways only dreamed of a few years ago. And this flood of options and information creates complexity. We must now choose from a growing number of possibilities and it is expected that we will make those choices faster so that we can keep up and not fall behind.

But there's a significant danger that lurks

beneath the surface of the technological world in which we live. People assume they can continue to make more decisions in less time and yet not sacrifice the quality of their decisions and, therefore, the quality of the outcomes. But it's just not true. And this kind of scenario has led to incredible confusion, frustration and anger.

Since depression is anger turned inward, is it any wonder in a time of unprecedented wealth, luxury and options that depression is the curse of our age? People in our culture increasingly resemble a child's pet hamster running madly on its wheel but getting nowhere.

So what is the answer to relativism and complexity? I believe the solution is to return to the absolute truth God has revealed to us in the Scriptures… truth that can light each step we take. We need *truth* in the face of relativism and we need the *light* it provides in response to the complexity that darkens our thinking.

That's the purpose of this series of 31 daily reflections. Taken from a group of Scripture verses that contain what I call God's "absolute" statements, they are designed to help light your way. These verses contain words such as *always*, *never*, *all*, *nothing*, and *impossible*. These are God's statements that leave no room for doubt and can't be explained away. They are clear and they apply all the time. Such statements by God represent the kind of sure-footed direction our souls need as we confront the spirit of our age.

Many of these verses will be well known to you, and there is a danger of equating long familiarity with constant practice. So as you read and meditate on these truths, I would like to challenge you to ask yourself two questions:

- Do I believe and appropriate this truth to its full extent?

● What would my life look like if I did?

One last note before we begin. All of these promises are for those who have chosen to receive and follow Christ as the savior and leader of their life. Here are a couple of "absolute" statements that speak to this subject (underlining is for emphasis):

Jesus answered, "I am the way and the truth and the life. No one comes to the Father except through Me" (John 14:6).

Yet to all who received Him, to those who believed in His name, He gave the right to become children of God (John 1:12).

"Behold I stand at the door and knock; if anyone hears My voice and opens the door, I will come in to him and will dine with him, and he with Me" (Revelation. 3:20, NASB).

If you have exercised your power of choice to follow Jesus Christ and have received His free gift of salvation, you are a child of God. All of these truths and promises are for those who have entered God's family. They are part of our inheritance.

My prayer is that you and I will learn to live the kind of life God has for us through the understanding and application of these treasures of truth.

Gregg Harris

All the days
ordained for me were
written in Your book
before one of them
came to be.

(Psalm 139:16)

Day One

GOD PLANNED ALL YOUR DAYS BEFORE YOU WERE BORN

You've heard it said that the best place to begin is at the beginning. In this case, however, we'll start *before* the beginning! Before you made your entrance on planet earth, God had ordained every one of your days. This is the kind of truth that takes some deep thinking to comprehend, and doing so can either upset us or comfort us.

Some might choose to be upset by the concept that this verse promotes a fatalistic view of our lives. They reason that if God has already planned all our days, then we don't have to take any initiative or responsibility for our lives. It's as if we are simply puppets that God has put on His stage and then does with as He pleases, regardless of our attitudes or efforts. This is an affront to our own natural understanding of the power of choice that

God has put within us.

But like many things in the universe, reality involves a delicate balance. Consider how God's creation requires precise tension between opposing forces.

- Scientists tell us that although we live millions of miles away from the sun, if there were to be less than a one percent change in that distance, it could result in drastic temperature shifts on earth.

- Our planet is rotating and floating through space at a speed of 18.5 miles per second, and yet the gravitational force of our sun keeps us from flying off into space.

- Our bodies have nine major systems and each of them must be in equilibrium for us to remain healthy.

- The ecosystem we live in is an intricate set

of forces that depend on each other for our world to properly function.

Since the finely tuned balance of tensions is a fundamental part of the physical universe, it is not surprising that the same is true in the spiritual realm. A fatalistic view of God's working does not reflect the Scriptural balance that exists between God's sovereign power and man's full responsibility to act within the boundaries of God's reign.

What then are we to take from this amazing statement? It seems that the intent of the writer of Psalm 139 was to convey the comforting thought of God's complete and intimate knowledge of each of His beloved creatures. Every one of the fifteen preceding verses of this psalm speaks in some way of God's thorough knowledge and involvement in our lives. In verse 6, the psalmist can hardly contain his emotions, "Such knowledge is too wonderful for me."

Wonderful is the appropriate description of this truth, because to be known so intimately and loved so tenderly is too marvelous for words. Few people in this world are thoroughly known and deeply loved by another human being. Those who receive the gift of human love experience a taste of heaven on earth. But everyone who belongs to God is completely known and perfectly loved.

If the God of the universe cares enough to write each of your days into His book before you draw your first breath, then your life is filled with meaning.

This knowledge is also too wonderful for us in the sense that we are not capable of comprehending it fully. Many aspects of God and His character are too great for us to understand. For this reason, theologians often divide God's attributes into two categories: communicable and incommunicable. Communicable attributes are those for which we have some frame of reference: mercy, kindness, goodness, and love. Incommunicable traits are those which are beyond our understanding: God is infinite, eternal, omnipresent, omnipotent and all-knowing. As finite human beings, we have no capacity to even begin to comprehend such traits.

When created beings encounter their Creator, there are always aspects of His person and work that defy our understanding. The appropriate response to these incomprehensible realities is humility and worship. So when God tells us that He has ordained all of our days before we were born, awe and gratitude should fill our hearts. As the psalmist said, "What is man that You are mindful of him, the Son of man that you care for him?" (Psalm 8:4).

You may not feel worthy of such loving attention, but that does not change the reality of God's devotion to you. If the God of the universe cares enough to write each of your days into His book before you draw your first breath, then your life is filled with meaning. And not just your life in the broad sense, but each and every day you have is a gift from God and has great meaning in His divine economy.

As you face each day, cling to this truth. Remember that this day was ordained for you by God. Remind yourself that He pays careful attention to each of your days because He loves you and has given you a part of His eternal plans. Live in the comfort and wonder of that love.

The Lord's
lovingkindnesses indeed
never cease,
for His compassions
never fail. They are new
every morning:
Great is Your faithfulness.

(Lamentations 3:22-23 NASB)

Day Two

GOD'S MERCY AND COMPASSION FOR YOU WILL NEVER CEASE OR FAIL

We started by reflecting on what happened before your life began… how God had already ordained each of your days. Now let's think about what happens at the beginning of each one of those God-ordained days. Every morning when you awake, God has prepared two new gifts for you to receive and enjoy: His lovingkindness and His compassion.

Most followers of Christ have heard much of God's lovingkindness and compassion, but too many of us have little understood or experienced their depth. If we view these aspects of God's character as static or fixed, they lose much of their power and compelling nature.

God is not a system or a set of propositional truths; He is a person. Nor is He a detached observer of the world. He did not set things in motion and then stand back to observe. And God is not a type of benevolent old man, a kind of heavenly grandfather, who possesses these "nice" traits. No, He is much more than any of these.

The God of the Bible is alive and powerful and dynamic. He is a Creator who is passionate about His work and is actively engaged in each of our lives. He is not only intimately involved in planning our lives, but He is also involved in restoring us when we fail. And we fail daily!

When you open your eyes in the morning, rejoice in the renewal of God's lovingkindness and tender compassion for you.

As a people, we excel at coming up with new ways to disobey God, to rebel, and to go our own way! But God has provided the answers to our varied and fresh failures. They are His daily lovingkindness and compassion. In one of the many paradoxes of

Scripture, it's the *renewal* of God's mercy that never changes. The Bible calls this His faithfulness.

Meditate on this magnificent truth. Each day when you awake, God stands ready to give you fresh grace and mercy. Think about how wonderful it is to know that no matter how we might have failed, each day God is renewing His mercy and grace.

Many of us who fail repeatedly begin to wonder if God tires of us and our failed ways. Does He grow weary of us because of our stubbornness, our pride, and our rebellion? According to this verse, He never tires of showing tenderness to us. Note that the words He uses to describe Himself are characterized by gentleness. This is not the kind of forgiveness granted with a sigh through clenched teeth. It is not a kind of cold discipline from a distant father who forgives us only because we're His children.

No, this is the infinite tenderness of a Father

who longs for His children to turn their hearts to Him. He wants us to enjoy the fruits of obedience to His will because it is the best path for us and it keeps us close to His heart. When we stray from that path, He aches for us to be reconciled. His love is so deep and infinite that it is renewed each morning as we come to Him with our need for grace, mercy and forgiveness.

I have often told people that, while I have a seminary degree, being a parent has taught me more about God's disposition toward us than all my theological studies. Being a father helps me understand the Father's heart. I understand in practical and daily terms what it means to love your child with new compassion and kindness each day. Yesterday's failures matter little to me when I see my daughter in the morning. I want to do everything in my power to help her grow and improve and experience all that is good in life. I have no interest in revisiting her past failures and reminding her of what is not right in her life. Each morning when I see

Rachel, I want to embrace her and tell her how much I love her and how glad I am that she is my child.

I assure you that I am not a perfect father. But even in my human weakness, I can understand the unfailing nature of the Father's love. Jesus expressed it well when He said, "If you, then, though you are evil, know how to give good gifts to your children, how much more will your Father in heaven give good gifts to those who ask Him!" (Matthew 7:11).

As you begin each day, develop the habit of consciously receiving these gifts. Embrace the fresh life and power that they bring. When you open your eyes in the morning, rejoice in the renewal of God's lovingkindness and tender compassion for you. God will continue to bring these gifts to you all day long. Fill your mind with the hope that when you wake tomorrow, He will be waiting with new mercies and kindness to shower upon you.

*J*esus replied:
"Love the Lord your God
with all your heart
and with all your soul
and with all your mind.
This is the first and greatest
commandment."

(Matthew 22:37-38)

Day Three

GOD WANTS YOU TO LOVE HIM WITH ALL YOUR BEING

We've established that God has ordained all our days, and that He provides fresh expressions of His mercy, love and kindness for each one of those days. But what does He want us to do with those days?

Here's where the trouble starts for most of us. We get confused about what God wants us to do. Or perhaps we have a sense of knowing what He wants us to do, but we find ourselves constantly failing to live up to that standard.

Many Christ followers develop a set of informal (but powerful) rules that govern their daily lives. These are the "should's" and "ought to's" which constantly voice their opinions. Inside our heads and often from our mouths, we hear things like: "A Christian should...." or "As a believer,

I ought to…." For many of us, these imperatives come straight out of the Bible, so they can't be wrong, can they? I hope I won't shock you by saying, "Yes they can… when they spring from the wrong motive."

The imperatives in the Bible always assume that we are acting out of love for God. In John 14:23 (NASB) Jesus said, "If anyone loves Me, he will keep My word." Which leads us to another biblical paradox: *Love will always yield obedience, but external obedience does not always indicate love.* This was the fundamental problem with the Pharisees, who received the harshest words of condemnation from Jesus during His time on earth.

The Pharisees were fanatically dedicated to understanding all of God's commands and obeying them. They hated Jesus because it seemed like He was telling people that it was wrong to obey God's laws (at least in the way the Pharisees understood them). Consider some of the questions the Pharisees asked Jesus and His disciples:

- *"Why are you doing what is unlawful on the Sabbath?"* (Luke 6:2).

- *"Why does your teacher eat with tax collectors and 'sinners'?"* (Matthew 9:11).

- *"Why do your disciples break the tradition of the elders? They don't wash their hands before they eat!"* (Matthew 15:2).

Before we are too hard on the Pharisees, let's remember that they honestly thought they were doing what was right. They believed they were promoting and teaching a life of total obedience to God's commands. But the Gospels make it clear that they were completely at odds with Jesus. The majority of Jesus' encounters with this group ended in conflict. What the Pharisees didn't understand is that God is totally opposed to external obedience which does not spring from a heart of love.

One day, one of the top experts in God's written Law tried to trap Jesus by asking Him: "Teacher, which is the greatest commandment in the Law?" Although this question was asked with evil intent, it is one of the most marvelous questions that could have ever been asked of Jesus. Because the answer to this question tells us God's most fundamental agenda for our lives.

No matter what form of obedience you bring to God, He is always looking beyond it to your heart. He wants to see the love and devotion behind the act, not the act itself.

Jesus said, "Love the Lord your God with all your heart and with all your soul and with all your mind" (Matthew 22:37). Don't let the familiarity of this statement hide its staggering implications. Think for a moment about what Jesus *could* have said in answer to this question. He could have talked about social justice, caring for the poor, offering worship, giving money, or any number of other emphases. But He told us once and for all that God's greatest desire is for us to love Him with every faculty we possess.

The God who created us knows that our capacity to love is the most powerful of all human endowments. He knows that when we love someone with all our being, everything else will fall into place around that person. Our energies, our attentions, our motivations, and our actions will all align themselves around the one we love. Obedience, service, and sacrifice all become easy when we love.

Fundamentally, there is only one "must" in the Christian life. We must love God with every fiber of our being. All our abilities must be directed to loving our heavenly Father. Anything less is disobedience. No matter what form of obedience you bring to God, He is always looking beyond it to your heart. He wants to see the love and devotion behind the act, not the act itself.

If you begin to take this command seriously and pursue it faithfully, you will find that many of your questions and confusions will melt away. Questions about God's will, about whether to take certain actions or to refrain from them, and other issues will resolve themselves as you lose yourself in devotion to the One who created you and who died for you and who loves you more than you can possibly comprehend.

Give yourself fully to God. Love Him with abandon. Make this the grand purpose of your life from this point forward. This is what you were created for. It is your destiny.

How precious it is,
Lord, to realize that You are
thinking about me constantly!
I can't even count how many
times a day Your thoughts
turn towards me.
And when I waken
in the morning,
You are still thinking of me!

(Psalm 139:17-18 LB)

Day Four

GOD IS ALWAYS THINKING ABOUT YOU

God has chosen to reveal Himself, His character and His feelings toward humanity through the Scriptures. This includes statements of His love for us, many of which are astonishing to consider. Today's verses represent one such statement.

Our Lord is often presented as a passionate lover, whose devotion to His beloved is extraordinary. One of the chief characteristics of people who are madly in love is that they think about each other all the time. Their thoughts are occupied constantly with the object of their affection. It gives them immense pleasure to reflect on the qualities of the one they adore. People hunger to be in this kind of love relationship.

Thousands of songs have been written celebrating the joy and ecstasy of that kind of love. But we all know from experience that human lovers often let each other down. And yet deep in our souls, each of us longs to experience the thrill of being deeply loved.

The answer to our longing is found not in fallible human love, but in the love of our Creator, who never changes and is perfect in every way. God is not subject to the daily ups and downs of emotions, fatigue or physical discomfort. His love for us is steady and unchanging. That is why the Bible uses metaphors of solidity and strength when describing God. He is given names like Rock, Strength, Fortress, Strong Deliverer and Shield. The depth of our longing to be loved is more than matched by God's capacity and desire to lavish His love upon us.

It is tremendously flattering to have someone pay attention to us. From early childhood, the desire manifests itself. Young children are constantly seeking the attention of their parents by saying,

"Look at me, Mommy!" or "Watch this, Daddy!" Children love to know they have an audience consisting of those they love. It satisfies their need for meaning and significance. The child reasons, "If Mom and Dad think I'm worth paying attention to, I must really be worthwhile."

Have you ever considered what it means to be loved by the almighty, all-knowing, all-powerful God of the universe? God created you. He knows you perfectly. He understands your strengths and your weaknesses. He sees you as you are. And yet, knowing all of that, He is passionately in love with you. The Bible says He thinks about you constantly! All day long, as you go about your daily affairs, the God of the universe is lovingly watching over you. When you awake each morning, He is still thinking about you.

I love to go into my daughter's room when she is asleep, gaze at her face, and pray for her.

I kiss her cheek, think about how much I adore her and how I long for her to experience a rich

The depth of our longing to be loved is more than matched by God's capacity and desire to lavish His love upon us.

and fruitful life. My heart overflows and feels like it will burst with joy. She is my child and I love her passionately. I would do anything for her, even protect her with my life. Your heavenly Father wants you to know that He watches over you with even greater care and constancy.

Some people find it difficult to comprehend or accept that God could love us in this way. They believe He is so far above us that He could not possibly exhibit such tender care. Many people view God as a kind of cold and impassive judge whose love for us is more like tolerance than warmth and devotion. Such understandings of God are common but misguided.

God has gone to great lengths to communicate the depth, strength and power of His love for us throughout the Bible. And because love always results in action, God expresses His love tangibly toward us. He even sacrificed His only Son on our behalf!

Our capacity to love is a dim reflection of God's pure and selfless love. And yet, God has been gracious enough to place in our hearts an understanding of what it means to love deeply. My commitment to my family is the most profound form of human love I have experienced. And although it is difficult for me to comprehend, God's love for me is deeper and stronger than the love I have for my wife and daughter. This is the kind of love you and I long for. There is an ache in our souls to have someone adore and embrace us this way.

How can we be worthy of such love? We can't. But we can respond to it with all our heart.

A true lover wants nothing more than to be loved in return. God does not require us to do anything to earn this love, but He does want us to respond with worship, gratitude and love. Don't try to earn God's love—it's impossible, because He has already given it freely to you. Instead, let the truth of His constant care for you overwhelm your heart until it overflows. As you do, you will begin to think about Him as often as He thinks about you.

*K*eep your lives free
from the love of money
and be content with what you have,
because God has said,
"Never will I leave you;
never will I forsake you."

(Hebrews 13:5)

Day Five

GOD WILL *NEVER* FORSAKE YOU

In 1854, Henry David Thoreau wrote, "The mass of men lead lives of quiet desperation."

A century and a half later, this statement still rings true. As I have traveled to many parts of the world, I have seen a common theme in the eyes of people from different countries and cultures. This thread which unites humanity is hopelessness and despair. Mother Theresa said, "The biggest disease today is not leprosy or tuberculosis, but rather the feeling of being unwanted."

What is at the root of this all too common human condition? I believe Mother Theresa identified it accurately. Few things bring on despair as quickly as the feeling of abandonment. To be left alone in the world with no present help and no hope for a future will lead most people into a state of desperation.

Those who do not believe in God have chosen a path of loneliness. Self-sufficiency may appeal to our vanity, but it does not satisfy the needs of the heart. As I Corinthians 10:12 says in *The Message*, "Forget about self confidence; it's useless. Cultivate God-confidence."

One of the most significant marks of Christ followers is that we not only have the hope of heaven, but we have the promise that God will never forsake us in this life. We may not be perfect, and our lives may be filled with trouble and difficulty, but we are not alone.

There will never be a single minute of your life when you will be abandoned by God.

When I was six years old, my family went on a vacation to Cape Cod, Massachusetts. One day, we went to the beach and swam in the ocean. As I came out of the water, I looked around and could not see my family. Fear swept over me as I scanned the beach desperately hoping to catch a glimpse of a familiar face. Panic set in and I began sprinting down the beach looking for my family. Unfortunately, I ran in the wrong direction.

What I didn't know was that my father and brother were keeping a close eye on me from a distance. They saw me come out of the water, look around and panic. Before they could get close enough to call out to me, I had taken off down the beach. They ran after me as fast as they could, but because I was so much lighter I moved more quickly over the sand. Fortunately, their persistence paid off and the pursuit ended in my retrieval.

Often we don't feel like God is watching over us. Sometimes when things are going badly for us, we even wonder if God has forsaken us. Many times, we act and speak as if God has abandoned us. We look anxiously at our circumstances and we don't see God. And we often respond by running for help in the wrong direction. But just because we don't see God doesn't mean He doesn't see us! Like my father and brother, He is watching us carefully and is ready to help us when we encounter trouble. He will even pursue us when we run away from Him.

At times like these, what we believe will show itself clearly in our actions. Because I believed my family had forsaken me, I ran desperately in search of help. Had I realized they could see me, even though I couldn't see them, I would have remained calm and waited for them to find me.

The next time you encounter difficulty, be aware of your reaction to it. Do you feel that God has forsaken you? Do you have an urge to run away? Even if you are filled with these emotions, God has given you the capacity to choose a different response based on the truths revealed in the Scriptures. The grammatical construction in Hebrews 13:5 contains five negatives which our English Bibles translate as "never, never." I had a seminary professor who said that the thrust of this text is more like this: God has said, "Never, never, never, never, never will I leave or forsake you!"

It is important to God that you and I know how absolute His commitment is to us. There will never be a single minute of your life when you will be abandoned by God. Things may look grim and bleak. Everything you depend on may let you down and disappoint you. But God is always there, watching, loving and waiting to help.

*C*ast all your anxiety on Him
because He cares for you.

(I Peter 5:7)

Day Six

GIVE GOD ALL OF YOUR CONCERNS, BECAUSE HE CARES FOR YOU

One of the fundamental truths of human existence is this: everyone has problems. To have problems means you are alive!

Have you ever wondered why it has to be this way? It's because we live in a fallen world, and yet we were created for an eternity of perfection. Deep in our souls, we have a strong sense of the need for "rightness" in our lives. We are keenly aware of the aspects of ourselves, others, and our environment which are not the way they should be. And when people and situations don't align with our ideals, we label them problems.

How do we respond to problems? Most people become anxious about them. This usually involves spending a good bit of time rehearsing in our minds what is wrong. Then we try to find the reasons for the problems. Finally we try to solve those problems based on our analysis of the situation and the tools at our disposal.

Different people choose different paths for dealing with their problems. Some tend to attack the problem head on with activity. Others take a more passive approach, choosing to do little or nothing in the hope that the problem will go away. Other people run away from their problems.

The reason we are to give God our problems is based on the unchanging truth that He cares for us.

What do you do with your problems? What approach do you take? Which method do you choose to deal with the things that you are most anxious about? God's Word tells us clearly what we are to do. Cast them on Jesus.

At first this may seem like an abstract instruction that is difficult to apply. How do you cast your cares on someone? But when you stop to think about it, we cast many potential anxieties or problems on people and institutions every day. The reason we don't think about it is that you and I choose to trust those on whom we throw those problems… and that act of faith relieves our anxieties.

Think about some of the basic issues of life. You need food and water. If either of these is impure, you could become ill and possibly die. Yet you ingest food and water from many sources each day without any anxiety because you trust that proper measures were taken to keep them pure.

You also need money and, like most people, you have to work hard to earn it. If your money were lost or taken from you, your life would be filled with anxiety. Yet you willingly take your paycheck and give it to the local bank, receiving only a piece of paper in return. You leave the bank without worry because you trust that they will keep your funds safe and return them to you when you want them.

It is our trust that relieves the worry and leaves us free from anxiety.

If we are so quick to entrust our problems to fallible men, why do we find it so difficult to cast our anxieties on Jesus? Is it because we can't see Him? Perhaps. But many of the systems and people we trust remain unseen to us. It may be that our struggle to trust God finds its roots in an inaccurate understanding of His character. Intellectually we know that God is all-powerful, but sometimes we find it difficult to see Him as loving and kind.

But the Bible makes it clear that the reason we are to give God our problems is based on the unchanging truth that He cares for us. When you know that someone loves you, it becomes easier to trust them.

I encourage you today to reflect deeply and often on God's tender care for you. Focusing on God's love for you will make it more natural for you to bring Him your anxieties and concerns. Begin to cultivate the habit of bringing God every problem and worry that you face. Think purposefully about coming before His throne and literally placing the situation into His outstretched hands. Then walk away, rejoicing that God will deal with the situation and resting in the knowledge that you don't need to handle it yourself.

*F*or the Lord
is always good.
He is always loving
and kind,
and His faithfulness
goes on and on
to each
succeeding generation.

(Psalm 100:5 LB)

Day Seven

GOD IS ALWAYS GOOD TO YOU

I once heard a prominent Christian leader make the following statement: "Your view of God determines absolutely everything in your life." The more I have reflected on this, the more I have understood the depth of its truth. Yet, many Christians give little or no attention to adjusting their view of God to ensure that it is accurate.

Imagine you woke up one morning and had difficulty seeing. Everything was blurry and you could see only large shapes and colors. You would have to feel your way around the house to get dressed and eat breakfast. You would be unable to drive or read or write. Your entire life would be in turmoil. In such a situation, most people would seek medical help immediately. They would do everything and anything required to regain the clarity of their vision. Why? Because without the ability to see the world around us clearly, everything becomes exponentially more difficult.

Everyone has a set of spiritual eyes through which they view the world. The accuracy of our vision in this area determines so much, and yet few people are even aware they have this capacity. But a lack of attention to your spiritual vision always has serious consequences.

Many Christ followers have developed views of God which are not compatible with what the Bible teaches. The implications of an inaccurate view of God are enormous, and yet we expend little effort developing an accurate understanding of God and correcting misconceptions about Him.

This verse from Psalm 100 provides great clarity in our understanding of God's character: He is *always* good, loving and kind. Many times when we are in the midst of hardship or suffering, we believe that God is not good. We become angry with Him and feel that He no longer loves us… that He somehow wants to be unkind to us. But those thoughts are not true! They represent a terrible blurring of our spiritual vision and will lead us to injure ourselves and others.

God's goodness, love and kindness are part of His character. He cannot be otherwise to His children. God does not change like you and I do, so the qualities of His character are permanent and must express themselves at all times. In every situation you encounter in life, God is being good to you. There is not a single second of your life in which God is not expressing His kindness to you. In every moment of your existence, God loves you with an unfailing and unconditional love.

The reason we often find it so difficult to embrace this truth about God is that it doesn't always feel true. But as important a role as emotions play in our lives, they are not trustworthy as a basis for making important decisions. A large part of maturity is the ability to subordinate our feelings to our commitments.

For example, an immature person wakes up in the morning and says, "I'm not going to work today because I don't feel like it." Such a person will eventually suffer the consequences of his immaturity. A mature person may wake up with the exact same feelings, but gets out of bed and goes to work anyway. That person does not live by the whims and dictates of his feelings. He understands that he has made a commitment to his job and has learned that there is greater value in honoring his commitments than allowing feelings to dictate how he acts.

In every moment of your existence, God loves you with an unfailing and unconditional love.

Everything that is worthwhile in your

life requires you to exercise some kind of self-control, including the control of your emotions. It's essential that you not allow your feelings to dictate how you act.

Someone at work makes you angry and your emotions tell you to physically injure them or to say something harsh to them. What would happen if you acted on those feelings without restraint? Or your child is sick in the middle of the night and wakes you up for help and comfort. The last thing you feel like doing is getting up. But you know what would happen if you left your child to fend for himself, so you ignore your feelings and do what needs to be done.

I hope you can see how important it is not to let your emotions tell you what is true. Never allow your feelings to rule your concept of God and His dealings with you. Make a commitment to give God's truth greater power in your life than your feelings.

Continually remind yourself that God always loves you with an unfailing love… every moment of every day. Absorb this truth until it seeps into the depths of your soul and begins to influence your entire outlook on life. Practice being aware that during each moment of your day, God is expressing His character to you through His goodness, love and kindness. Then thank Him for His faithfulness to you and embrace the grace that He bestows upon you.

*Therefore, there is now
no condemnation
for those who are
in Christ Jesus.*

(Romans 8:1)

Day Eight

AS A CHRIST FOLLOWER, YOU ARE NO LONGER UNDER GOD'S CONDEMNATION

Many of us as Christians spend a great deal of our time and energy feeling guilty. We are experts at condemning ourselves.

Could it be that we secretly believe that it is not only acceptable, but good for us to condemn ourselves for our wrong thoughts and actions? After all, doesn't God hate sin? Of course, He does! So when we sin, isn't it okay for us to be hard on ourselves, to tear ourselves down for our unfaithfulness and rebelliousness?

No—it's not! Or as the apostle Paul would say, "May it never be!"

Condemnation means that you are judged guilty and sentenced to pay for what you've done. It means you have been declared in violation of the law and you must be punished. The Bible makes it clear that those who follow Christ have had the price paid for *all* of their sins. There is not a single sin you will ever commit for which you will have to make any kind of payment.

Ephesians 1:4 says, "For He chose us in Him before the creation of the world to be holy and blameless in His sight." You cannot be mostly holy, or almost blameless. The apostle Paul tells us in this verse that you and I as Christ followers have experienced a complete cleansing from sin and guilt. Every act of disobedience you have committed or will commit has already been paid for, and you are completely free from condemnation!

Some of you are reading these words and saying, "Yes, I know all this. I've heard it for years." Others are saying, "This sounds too good to be true. It seems too easy." But my question to you is this: Do you really understand what it means to be free from all condemnation? Are you living out the implications of this amazing truth? Are you depriving God the gratitude and love which He deserves for paying all of your debts? Or are you trying to pay for that which God has already paid? Do you understand that when you condemn yourself you are distracted from receiving God's love? Do you recognize that when you try to pay for your sins you essentially reject God's gift to you?

Imagine the following scenario: A young girl has a habit of disobeying her father in ways which end up costing money. She breaks her neighbor's window after he tells her not to play ball near their house. She rides her bike through their flowerbeds. She destroys decorative items in the house by playing with them after being told not to. After each occurrence, she comes to her father and tells him how sorry she is for her disobedience. She is guilty and she needs to pay for what she has done. But he knows that she is unable to pay for her transgressions. He is a poor man, but he has one item of great value—his grandfather's gold watch. His great love for his child leads him to sell the precious family heirloom for $10,000 and place the money in a special account to pay for everything she has broken or will break. He tells her what he has done and now she knows there will be more money in the account than she will ever need to pay for the consequences of her disobedience.

Every act of disobedience you have committed or will commit has already been paid for, and you are completely free from condemnation!

Isn't that a ridiculously extravagant gesture on the father's part? Yes, but God's love for us is even more extravagant. Did the girl's father need to pay such a price for her wrongdoings? No, but he did it gladly because his love for her knows no bounds. But how would he feel if after telling her what he's done, she rejects his generosity because she says she can take care of herself? His heart would be grieved because she would not receive his expression of love. Might she not respond to his generosity by being more careless and breaking things with impunity because they're already paid for? Yes, but he is willing to take that chance because those who love always risk being taken advantage of by those they love.

What then is his object and desire in doing something like this? As a father, he wants nothing more than to express his love to his child and to receive love in return. Imagine, if in response to this act of great love, the little girl's heart is filled with love and gratitude. Every day she expresses her appreciation to her father for his kindness and generosity. The more she thinks about it, the more deeply she understands his love for her and what he sacrificed for her. Her own love for and dedication to her father grows. She knows that her every mistake will be paid for from her father's provision, but rather than abusing the privilege, she wants more than anything to obey him and not draw upon the account. She uses her security to devote her energies to pleasing him rather than trying to pay for her wrongdoing. When she does fail and money must be paid from the account, she is reminded again of what he has done for her and how much he loves her. Everything she does, both good and bad, reminds her of her father's love. And her father's heart overflows with joy, and he never once regrets the sacrifice he made.

Child of God, your Father loves you more than you can possibly imagine. Your sins are paid for. He gladly sacrificed that which is most precious to Him in order to express His love for you. He does not expect or want you to pay for your sins. He longs for you to understand the depth and intensity of His devotion to you, and wants nothing more than for you to live each moment in the wonder of His love, giving all of your love to Him in return.

And without faith
it is impossible to please God,
because anyone who comes to Him
must believe that He exists
and that He rewards those
who earnestly seek Him.

(Hebrews 11:6)

Day Nine

IT IS IMPOSSIBLE TO PLEASE GOD IF YOU DON'T TRUST HIM

There are many things in our lives that require one small but important factor to release a very substantial set of benefits.

Imagine, if in one day, you lost all of your keys and forgot all of your passwords. You would be unable to get into your house and rest comfortably. You would have no protection from the elements and you wouldn't be able to get any money as your ATM card wouldn't work. You wouldn't be able to log on to the internet or access your email. And you would be locked out of your car and have to walk everywhere.

Such scenarios are unthinkable because to live our lives without keys and passwords would be terribly impractical, if not impossible.

Keys and passwords are so small and simple–just pieces of metal and sets of numbers or letters. Yet possessing and using them has an enormous impact on how we live our lives. We understand their importance in the physical realm, yet we frequently ignore some of the keys which God has given us. Is it because they seem too small, too simple, and too obvious? Whatever the reason, many Christians stand outside the abundant life they desire, looking longingly at the comforts, joys and blessings inside and wondering what they must do to gain access.

If you want to enter into the delightful condition of being pleasing to the God of the universe, there is one key: faith.

This verse is one of the most straightforward statements in the Bible. If you want to enter into the delightful condition of being pleasing to the God of the universe, there is one key: faith. It's impossible to get into this place without that key, yet many people struggle to gain a clear understanding of faith. It seems that they stumble over the simplicity of the concept.

Faith means you have confidence that someone can be trusted to do what he says he will do. In the Bible, God is quite specific about what He will do. He promises to forgive your sins, give you eternal life, guide you, provide for you, and protect you. And there are many more promises He makes, but the key to accessing all of those benefits is faith. He asks that you put your confidence in Him, and this simple key is what opens the treasury of heaven to you.

God wants to be trusted! He is greatly pleased when we trust Him, and if we try to please Him without trusting Him, we'll be locked out! Even as a fallible human being, I am very pleased when someone trusts me. To be trusted is to have someone speak well of my character and my competence.

Over and over again in the Scriptures, we see God as a relational being. His overriding interest is relationships, not rules or scorecards or measures of any kind. And when you and I put our confidence in God, we are telling Him, ourselves, and the world around us that He is good, that His character and competence make Him worthy of our trust.

This kind of trust is so important to God that He promises to reward those who believe He exists and who act on that belief by earnestly seeking Him. This is not about earning points with God—it is about being in a loving and trusting relationship with Him. The more we understand His character, the more we love Him. As we grow to love Him, we come to understand His competence, and we realize we can trust Him. The more we trust Him, the more we please Him. The more we please Him, the more He rewards us. True to His character, God creates a system of abundance where everybody wins. He even puts the keys in our hands and tells us how to use them to our benefit.

Are you taking every opportunity you can to trust God? Are you looking for practical ways each day to let God know you trust Him? Are you meditating on the beauty of His character and the awesome nature of His power until you find it a privilege to entrust every aspect of your life to Him? If you are, then you are using your key to open the door to a life that is pleasing to God.

" And I will do
whatever you ask in My name,
so that the Son may bring glory
to the Father.
You may ask Me for anything
in My name,
and I will do it."

(John 14:13-14)

Day Ten

YOU CAN ASK JESUS FOR ANYTHING IF YOU DO SO IN HIS NAME

I carry two credit cards in my wallet. One is for my personal expenses and the other is a corporate card owned by FEBC, the ministry I work for.

No matter where I am in the world, when I pull out the corporate card, I can buy anything in the name of FEBC. Sounds pretty exciting, doesn't it? Perhaps. But it all depends on a clear understanding of what the phrase "in the name of FEBC" means. Let's think this phrase through, because it will help us understand the meaning of these verses.

FEBC is a ministry with specific purposes and it has resources available to accomplish those purposes. As one of the leaders of the ministry, I am given access to and responsibility for the proper use of those resources. So what prevents me from using these resources to satisfy all my own desires and whims? It's that little phrase, "in the name of FEBC."

Anyone who is given a corporate credit card receives clear instructions that it is only to be used for approved ministry expenses. I can use my corporate card to purchase anything that falls within the approved budget, because that budget represents

God seeks obedient servants, not editors of His divine directions!

the will of the ministry. When I am accomplishing the will of the ministry, I have authorization to use its resources.

In John 14, Jesus is giving us the same kind of authority. He is telling us that we are authorized to have access to all of His resources as long as we are using them to accomplish His plans and purposes. Throughout the book of John, Jesus stated that His purpose was not to do His own will. His sole concern was His Father's will. This is why Jesus had access to all of God's power and resources. In John 14:10 Jesus said, "The words I say to you are not just My own. Rather, it is the Father, living in Me, who is doing His work."

Much of our struggle in the area of prayer has to do with our will. We often come to God with a laundry list of our wants and desires. While Philippians 4:6 says "Let your requests be made known to God (NASB)," all of the Bible's teaching on prayer is set in the context of a spirit of submission to God's will. Jesus Christ is our supreme example. At His hour of greatest suffering, He told God what was in His heart, but then said, "... not My will but Yours be done."

Many people come to God in prayer asking Him to reveal His will to them. But in their hearts, they want to evaluate what He asks them to do and then decide if they will obey. This is *not* what it means to ask in Jesus' name. God seeks obedient servants, not editors of His divine directions! To ask for something in Jesus' name is to seek to accomplish what Jesus wants, not to forward our own agenda.

Do you want God to answer your prayers? Does the idea of coming to God's throne and receiving anything you ask for excite you? Then set your heart and mind to want nothing more than His will. If your chief aim is to accomplish God's purposes and bring Him glory, you will be able to ask for anything and God will give it to you.

One note of caution: Be careful not to depersonalize this promise. God is not some kind of cosmic vending machine, impersonally dispensing gifts and resources. If you receive this promise as a way to get what you want without engaging in an intimate relationship with your heavenly Father, you will be sorely disappointed. The root of our connection with Him is the deep and unconditional love which flows eternally from His heart. Everything He does toward us is an expression of that love, including the answers He gives to our prayers. Approach Him with loving reverence, desiring to please Him and to accomplish His purposes. You will be amazed to see Him move heaven and earth to answer your prayers.

*B*e joyful always;
pray continually;
give thanks in all circumstances,
for this is God's will for you
in Christ Jesus.

(1 Thessalonians 5:16-18)

Day Eleven

GOD DESIRES FOR YOU TO LIVE A LIFE THAT IS CHEERFUL, PRAYERFUL AND THANKFUL ALL THE TIME

Many of the commands in Scripture run against the grain of human nature. It is our natural tendency to complain, to focus on what's wrong in our circumstances, and to resist seeking God's help.

What is striking about the commands in these verses is not only how contrary they are to our natural tendencies, but how they are to be applied at *all* times. The strength and clarity of these imperatives is hard to ignore.

God makes it abundantly clear in these brief statements that it is His intention for us to be joyful, prayerful and thankful in *every* circumstance we face in life. This means that in God's eyes there is never a legitimate reason for us to be otherwise.

In our hearts, we rebel against such a suggestion. After all, it seems so unreasonable! How can we possibly obey such a set of commands? Why can't we indulge our natural inclinations of complaining, negative thinking and self-sufficiency? Quite simply, because God created us and knows what is best for us.

As a parent, I have spent many years teaching my daughter to do things which are not natural to her: going to bed early, eating the right kinds of food, not running out into the street, being generous and considerate of others. Over the years, she has grown to understand how much I want what is best for her. Although it is still not easy for her, she knows in her heart that even when I ask her to do something difficult, I am always seeking her highest good. If a child can learn to trust an imperfect parent, surely you and I can learn to trust our perfect heavenly Father!

God's will, as expressed in these commands, is for our good and the prosperity of our souls. Set aside for a moment the difficulty of constant obedience to them, and imagine what your life would be like if you lived this way. Your heart would be filled with joy all the time... you would be grateful in every circumstance you encountered... and your focus would be on the things for which you were thankful. You would live each moment in loving communion with God and experience His presence continually.

In short, you would be blessed, peaceful and happy. Can you see why God desires this kind of life for His children?

But how can we do this? First, we must not view these commands as tasks to be undertaken apart from our relationship with God. It is not possible to live this way in our own strength. We are not being exhorted to some form of positive thinking exercise. Rather, these commands paint a picture of life lived in a vital, dynamic relationship with Christ.

Be joyful always. Constant joy cannot come from our circumstances; it can only come from a love relationship with Jesus Christ. A person who has just fallen in love is happy in spite of their circumstances. Why? Because their constant focus is on the one they love and who loves them. They meditate on the pleasure of loving and being loved. This leads them to feel and express the joy of their relationship, even when other more unpleasant things are happening in their lives. God wants us to live this way. The Bible's exhortations for us to rejoice are almost always linked to our relationship with God. His goodness, faithfulness, generosity and love are the wellspring of our joy. As we learn to turn our thoughts toward the realities of a never-ending love

God's will... is for our good and the prosperity of our souls.

relationship with the Creator of the universe, we will experience increasingly deeper levels of joy.

Pray without ceasing. There is really only one way to realize a life of prayer without ceasing. It begins with a desire to allow Christ's life to flow through us on a moment by moment basis, followed by a commitment to surrender our life to God's control. It is actualized as we begin to practice God's presence throughout the day. As we do these things, we find our hearts turning to God more and more consistently in a spirit of gratitude and supplication. We can become like Frank Laubach, founder of World Literacy Crusade, who in 1930 began a personal discipline of turning his thoughts to Christ for one second every minute. This simple exercise changed his life and ministry, and, brought Him more joy than he could ever have dreamed.

In everything give thanks. Most of us recognize the happiness and contentment we would experience if we were more grateful. Something in our nature seems to make us focus on what's wrong with our lives, rather than what is good and right. God gives us no wiggle room here when He tells us that as His followers, we need to be thankful in every circumstance we encounter. What do we do when things happen that we are not thankful for? If someone we love becomes seriously ill, are we to be thankful? If we lose our job, are we to be filled with gratitude? The difficult answer is yes. But we are not to be thankful *for* the bad things that occur. Rather our gratitude stems from the fact that Christians never suffer without hope. Even when terrible things happen in our lives, we know that God loves us and will ultimately bring good out of pain and suffering.

These commands represent a challenging and exciting way to live our lives before God. If you did nothing more than apply these simple truths in your walk with Christ, you would experience a level of intimacy with God that would change your world forever.

And we know
that in all things
God works for the good
of those who love Him,
who have been called
according to
His purpose.

(Romans 8:28)

Day Twelve

GOD WORKS FOR YOUR GOOD IN ALL CIRCUMSTANCES

This is one of the great promises of the Bible. It is well loved by Christians and even many non-Christians are familiar with it.

These few words present a powerful truth that has comforted millions in times of darkness and distress. Before we meditate on the promise and seek to enjoy its benefits, let's deal with a few potential misunderstandings which can rob us of its power.

First, the promise is not for everyone. As the passage clearly states, God does this great work *only* for those who love Him and who are called according to His purpose. God respects each person's right to choose their response to Him and experience the subsequent consequences. Freedom without consequences is no freedom at all. Those who choose not to submit themselves to God do not enjoy all of the benefits of His specific care and protection. There is nothing harsh or cruel in this statement; on the contrary, it shows that God treats us with great respect.

Second, this verse is not saying that God will make everything turn out all right here on earth (at least according to our definition). God does not promise us that every tragedy will have a happy ending or that all suffering will be eliminated. If this promise is viewed only in terms of our earthly existence, we will often be disappointed. In many cases, it can only be understood in the light of eternity.

Finally, we are not being told that everything that happens to us is good. The Scriptures are clear that the world we live in is in rebellion against God and that much of what happens to us is caused either by evil or by human selfishness. The painful events of our lives are not good in themselves.

So how are we to understand this promise? Perhaps a simple illustration will help. Imagine that you are very hungry and your friend invites you to his home with the promise of preparing something to satisfy your hunger. He tells you that he has an exciting recipe he wants to share with you. You sit down to his table and he brings out a bowl of butter! He encourages you to enjoy it, and not wishing to offend him, you try to stomach a small amount. He returns from the kitchen again and enthusiastically presents you with some raw eggs. Again, you ingest his offering with some difficulty. Next he brings out a bowl of sugar. While this tastes much better, it is still difficult to eat much of it. The process continues with a large serving of dry flour, followed by small amounts of salt, baking powder and vanilla extract. You go home unsatisfied, still hungry, and exhausted from the effort of trying to eat such a strange meal. Imagine how different your experience would have been if your friend had combined all of these disparate ingredients in the proper amounts and baked you a cake!

What God promises to do with the events of our lives (particularly the difficult ones) is to combine them in ways which yield something far different and more pleasant than they could ever be by themselves. Often, we are able to see and enjoy God's redemptive work in our lives here on this earth. And one of the most striking features of Christ followers is that they can experience a painful event and afterwards say that they would go through it again if they had the choice.

We know that under God's loving care there are no accidents; nothing catches Him by surprise.

Does this mean that Christians have some strange love of pain? Certainly not! They understand how God worked through something terrible and used it to bring a harvest of spiritual growth. As a result, they would rather have both the growth *and* the pain, than have neither.

While we often focus on the ways in which God brings about good in our earthly life, there is another dimension we cannot ignore. We were created for eternity and our time on earth is an indescribably tiny fraction of our overall existence. Throughout the Bible we are taught that there will be eternal rewards for those who love and follow Christ. Romans 8:18 says, "I consider that our present sufferings are not worth comparing with the glory that will be revealed in us." The implication of this is that many of the difficult things that happen to us on earth are intended for our eternal good. We may see some benefit here in this life, but it is quite plausible that we will not enjoy or understand the real good until our earthly life is over.

In either case, we can embrace this truth

and apply it to every circumstance we face in life. It gives us hope and joy in the midst of great difficulty, because we know that our loving God is taking even unpleasant circumstances and working them out for a greater purpose. This brings a kind of deep joy and contentment to us, no matter what is happening around us. We know that under God's loving care there are no accidents; nothing catches Him by surprise. This knowledge gives us the courage to face whatever life holds for us. Since there are no exceptions to this promise, we can claim its truth and power each moment of our lives.

*C*onsider it pure joy,
my brothers,
whenever you face trials
of many kinds, because you know
that the testing of your faith
develops perseverance.
Perseverance must finish its work
so that you may be mature and
complete, not lacking anything.

(James 1:2-4)

Day Thirteen

LEARN TO REJOICE WHENEVER YOU FACE TRIALS

There are few imperatives in Scripture that are more contradictory to our natural inclinations than this one. We want to be comfortable, pain-free, prosperous and secure. We do not want to encounter difficulties and trouble, and when we do, everything within us shouts, "This is not fair! This should not be happening to me!"

But as with so many things in life, God has a different perspective—one that is based on His knowledge of our needs as seen in the light of eternity.

This command is not suggesting that all Christ followers become pain lovers. Nothing in the Bible suggests that we should seek out pain and difficulty. On the contrary, trouble finds us. Job 5:7 states, "Yet man is born to trouble as surely as sparks fly upward." Jesus Himself said, "Each day has enough trouble of its own" (Matthew 6:34).

Our Lord clearly did not intend His followers to seek pain. He was stating the reality that all human beings will experience trouble in their lives. So, it is not the pain we love, but rather the results that come when we allow the pain to teach us. For those who are willing to learn, pain and difficulty are master teachers.

There is a danger that we might dismiss this command as unrealistic. How can we consider troubles and hardship to be pure joy? Upon further reflection we find that it is not unrealistic at all. We are simply being exhorted to understand and obey the principles of discipline which apply to almost any endeavor.

In order to achieve mastery in a specific field, a person must submit himself to the time-tested training methods of that discipline. Such approaches are proven to lead people to the skills and qualities they are seeking to acquire. Athletes engage in rigorous physical training and many forms of self-denial in order to be able to perform at the highest levels. Artists submit to apprenticeship and constant practice of their craft in order to achieve the proficiency which allows them to fully express their creativity. In each of these examples, those seeking mastery are willing to do things which are laborious, difficult and often painful in order to reach their goal.

As followers of Christ, it is our goal to please our Master through loving surrender of our lives to His eternal purposes. God's great purpose is that His followers "be conformed to the likeness of His Son" (Romans 8:29). The path to this great destiny is filled with difficulties. You and I cannot be made like Jesus by having a trouble-free existence. If we think otherwise, we will be disappointed, frustrated, and more importantly, we will never fulfill God's purposes for our lives.

Perhaps you are like me in wishing that we could grow without difficulty and pain. However, our character never grows through ease, but only through suffering and hardship. C.S. Lewis wrote, "God whispers to us in our pleasures, speaks in our conscience, but shouts in our pains: it is His megaphone to rouse a deaf world." We cannot change the truth of these principles, but we can choose how we respond to them. We can opt out of God's training program by seeking relief and escape from trouble, or we can give ourselves fully to God's purpose by letting our troubles become our teachers.

> *As Christ followers, we need to learn to "lean into" our difficult circumstances, even though it seems unnatural to us.*

Some years ago, I went whitewater rafting for the first time. Before we entered the water, our guide gave us an instruction that did not make sense to a group of beginners. He said that if the raft was about to run into a large rock or boulder, everyone should lean into it rather than away from it. Some of us began to wonder if this man was an expert, because that sounded like the wrong way to deal with a potentially dangerous situation.

The four people in my raft learned our lesson a short time later. We were careening down the river through some rapids and our raft headed straight for a large boulder. Instinctively, we all leaned away from the rock, and before we knew what was happening, the front of the raft slid up on the rock and water came flooding in the back. We were fortunate not to capsize the boat entirely. Had we understood and applied our guide's instruction (which we did the next time) we would have seen the boat simply bounce off the rock and proceed safely down the river.

As Christ followers, we need to learn to

"lean into" our difficult circumstances, even though it seems unnatural to us. When problems arise, rather than shy away, we should embrace them as opportunities to build our character. Approaching our troubles this way will build strength and security, and most importantly, it will help us become more like Christ. This is why we are told to consider it "pure joy" when we encounter trials. The joy comes from the end result, even though the process may involve pain. This teaching is not for the faint of heart. It is advanced, high level training in the Christian life, but its application will lead you to the freedom and joy that each one of us longs for.

*D*o nothing
out of selfish ambition
or vain conceit,
but in humility consider others
better than yourselves.
Each of you
should look not only to
your own interests,
but also to the interests of others.
Your attitude should be the same
as that of Christ Jesus.

(Philippians 2:3-5)

Day Fourteen

DO NOTHING FROM SELFISHNESS

Selfishness is one of the earliest traits to express itself in the life of every human being. The moment a baby enters the world, all its energies are devoted to satisfying its own needs and desires.

Of course, there is nothing fundamentally wrong with this, because babies are not capable of caring for themselves or providing for the needs of others. However, over the ensuing years it is expected that the child will develop the willingness and ability to respect and serve the needs of others. It is assumed that along with physical maturity will come emotional maturity… the ability to subordinate selfish impulses to higher values.

Selflessness is highly prized by Christians and non-Christians alike. People who display selflessness are admired and held up as models for others to follow. Why? Because there is something attractive about a person who willingly sacrifices his or her own desires in order to serve another. When we see loving self-denial, it connects with our ideals of what we were created to be. We recognize that if more people were less selfish, the world would be a much better place.

But as compelling as these reasons are, for Christ followers there are deeper reasons to pursue this ideal.

Our motivation to be free of selfishness comes from our desire to become more like our Lord. The attitude we are exhorted to have is the same attitude Jesus had when He left heaven to become a man. The verses in Philippians 2 that follow those above, describe what is known in theological terminology as the *kenosis* of Jesus. *Ekenosen* is the Greek word often translated as "emptied," and it describes beautifully what Jesus did by choosing to leave the glory of heaven for the harsh realities and limitations of humanity. Because of His great selflessness and the noble purpose of saving humanity from its sins, Jesus emptied Himself completely and took on a human form. For the God of the universe, the One through whom everything was created, this was a sacrifice beyond our comprehension.

Jesus Christ is the supreme example of selflessness.

Consider your own life and ask yourself what "emptying" needs to occur. What thoughts, attitudes or actions do you cherish that only serve your selfish desires? What do you need to release in order to look out for the interests of others?

If this seems too difficult, let me encourage you with another one of the great paradoxes of Scripture: We never give something up without gaining even more in return. Our God is so good and His love for us is so great that even when He asks us to deny ourselves, He stands ready to bless us in even greater measure.

In Luke 9:24 Jesus said, "For whoever wants to save his life will lose it, but whoever loses his life for Me will save it." In Luke 6:38 Jesus said, "Give, and it will be given to you. A good measure, pressed down, shaken together and running over, will be poured into your lap. For with the measure you use, it will be measured to you."

As we surrender our self-centered desires and submit ourselves to His will, we enter a place of indescribable freedom.

It is a law of the Kingdom of God that no one can out give the King. While sacrifice is not easy, God never commands it simply to see us struggle or squirm. The sacrifices He requires of us are intended to bring us to a place of greater maturity and blessing.

While selfishness is natural to us, it is not good for us. God's command to abandon a self-centered life is about freedom. Selfishness represents a kind of bondage, an enslavement to our desires. Our Lord wants us to learn how liberating it is to lose our life to Him. As we surrender our self-centered desires and submit ourselves to His will, we enter a place of indescribable freedom.

Imagine being free from self-concern; having the ability to think foremost of God's will and the good of others. Consider being unfettered by the need to protect yourself and the image that others have of you! Think about the courage which would grow in you as you are able to do what is right without worrying about its impact on your personal interests.

This is the life God is calling you to. Is it possible? Jesus Christ has proven that it is. He is calling you and me to follow in His footsteps; to leave behind the bondage of selfishness and enter into the joy of a life lived for God and for others.

*T*rust in the LORD
with all your heart
and lean not
on your own understanding;
in all your ways acknowledge Him,
and He will
make your paths straight.

(Proverbs 3:5-6)

Day Fifteen

TRUST GOD FULLY WITH EVERY PART OF YOUR LIFE

One of the most prominent themes in Scripture is the absolute primacy God places on the importance of trusting Him. Throughout the Bible we are urged to place our confidence in God.

It appears that God knows we need many reminders of such an important aspect of our relationship with Him. And because He understands our nature and tendencies, He has seen fit to ensure there is no ambiguity on this one point: He wants us to trust Him!

Every command God gives us must be understood in the light of our relationship to Him. When we view His commands as simply matters of our behavior, apart from our vital connection to our Lord, we miss the point.

God has revealed Himself primarily as a lover of His human creatures. As a lover, He pursues His beloved and His main concern is the response from the object of His affection. You may already be familiar with this concept and will want to move on to something deeper or more novel. But stop for a moment to consider how extraordinary this is.

To trust in the Lord with all your heart means to give yourself unreservedly to His purposes in your life.

Throughout human history, men have had thousands of gods. Almost every deity created by man is feared by its worshippers and demands some form of appeasement. The relationship between god and worshipper is almost always defined by the worshipper making himself acceptable to the god. In many cases the primary objective is to prevent the god from becoming angry and punishing its subjects. The constant cry of the worshipper is, "Please don't reject me! Please tell me I'm acceptable!"

What a contrast this is to the relationship we have with the one true God through Jesus Christ! Rather than demanding that we make ourselves acceptable to Him, He sacrificed His Son to make us worthy. Rather than requiring us to obey a set of laws to satisfy Him, He asks for our love and trust. When we consider what a privilege it is to have the God of the universe pursue us in love, His command to trust Him with all our heart seems only natural.

The scope of this command is quite clear. God wants *all* your heart *all* the time.

To trust in the Lord with all your heart means to give yourself unreservedly to His purposes in your life. It means telling God that you want His will more than your own because you are convinced He knows what is best for you.

Partial trust is a contradiction in terms. Trust that is genuine involves leaning fully on the object that is being trusted. God states clearly that we are not to put our trust in our own understanding. He knows our natural inclination is to trust our own judgment. When we are under pressure, we try to figure out our problems and come up with human solutions. But many situations we face in life defy human ingenuity and require divine intervention. Which is why, when you face such situations, God calls you to lean completely on Him for the answers you need.

To acknowledge God in all your ways means that each event of your life is lived in light of His love for you. It means that you cultivate the habit of turning your thoughts to God as you face your daily responsibilities and challenges. As you develop the regular practice of relying on God rather than your own wisdom, you will experience the joy of having Him "direct your paths." You will see Him intervene in your circumstances in ways too clear to deny. He will give you insights which you know are beyond your human ability. He will bring about results that far exceed any you could produce yourself.

In short, you will become a vessel through whom God will accomplish His purposes.

Begin to view each situation you face as an opportunity to lean on God. As you go through your day, consciously acknowledge His love and lordship in your life. Expect Him to guide you and trust wholeheartedly in His ability to do so. As you progress in these practices, you will experience the joy of the Lord flowing through your life and it will spill over into the lives and hearts of those around you.

*P*raise be
to the God and Father
of our Lord Jesus Christ,
the Father of compassion
and the God of all comfort,
who comforts us
in all our troubles,
so that we can comfort those
in any trouble with the comfort
we ourselves have received
from God.

(2 Corinthians 1:3-4)

Day Sixteen

YOU CAN COUNT ON GOD'S COMFORT IN EVERY TROUBLE YOU FACE

Life is full of trouble. No one seems to have a shortage of problems and struggles. While people often go through periods where everything goes smoothly, such seasons rarely last for long.

The Bible does not ignore these realities; rather it speaks directly to them and shows us how to conduct ourselves in the real world.

What most of us want and need when we are having difficulty is some kind of comfort. Our problems are like wounds to our soul and we often look for ways to medicate ourselves. Look around you and observe all the ways people seek relief from their problems: drugs, alcohol, food, sex, achievement, power, money and the acquisition of possessions. People often seek after these things as the central purpose of their lives. Their credo is "you only go around once, so get all the pleasure and enjoyment you can from life."

God knows our lives are filled with trouble. He knows that we need comfort and He knows how prone we are to seek it anywhere but from Him. That's why this passage from 2 Corinthians is so important as it reveals some profound truths about our Father's love for us.

Today, I want you to take courage in the knowledge that God is always there when you are in pain, His arms outstretched, ready to give you the comfort you long for.

First, He is described as the Father of compassion. What a wonderful description! Our God is not harsh, cold and unsympathetic to our struggles. Hebrews 4:15 says, "For we do not have a high priest who is unable to sympathize with our weaknesses, but we have one who has been tempted in every way, just as we are—yet was without sin." Jesus Christ understands what it is like to be human, and He empathizes with our struggles as we face life's challenges.

Second, our Lord is described as the God of all comfort. He is not the God of *some* comfort, or *little* comfort, but **all** comfort. He comforts us in **all** our troubles. This is a promise with no exceptions. No matter what kind of trouble you are facing, God will comfort you if you will let Him.

Consider for a moment how significant this is. In every problem you face, in every hurt you feel, and in every disappointment you have, God stands ready to give you comfort.

Perhaps you are saying to yourself, "I have been through many problems in my life and there are times when God hasn't given me comfort." This is an honest statement that applies to many of us. And it is true that we do not always receive comfort from God when we are in pain. But the reason we don't receive that comfort is not because God is unwilling to give it. He is always there for us… but we do not always turn our hearts to Him.

We are like a person who claims that radio waves do not exist because we are unwilling to turn on our radio!

Today, I want you to take courage in the knowledge that God is always there when you are in pain, His arms outstretched, ready to give you the comfort you long for. His heart is filled with compassion and love for you. He does not want you to suffer alone and He wants to help you. Your part is to turn to Him for comfort, to "tune your heart" to receive His grace.

Throughout the Bible, God is referred to as a shelter or a fortress in times of trouble. This familiar metaphor helps us to see our part in receiving help and comfort from God. If you are near a fortress and you are attacked, your response is evident and simple: you rush into it and stay there. By doing this, you put the fortress between you and your attackers and you are protected by its strength.

Anyone who was being attacked and refused to go into the nearby shelter for protection would be regarded as foolish. Yet we often fail to run to the shelter of God's protection. Instead, we run to other shelters to seek relief from our troubles. Many of these fortresses appear to be quite secure, but their strength is an illusion. There is only one sure source of help: The Father of compassion and the God of all comfort.

When troubles come your way, imagine yourself running into the safety of your Father's arms. Recognize the temptation to turn to other sources of protection, and remind yourself that in spite of their attractiveness, none of them can truly protect or comfort you. Envision God as a solid fortress that you can enter into and stay near in order to receive protection from your hurts and pains. Allow Him to give you the comfort you need exactly at the time you need it.

And my God
will meet all your needs
according to His glorious riches
in Christ Jesus.

(Philippians 4:19)

Day Seventeen

GOD WILL MEET EVERY ONE OF YOUR NEEDS

There are certain promises in Scripture which are staggering in their content yet understated in their wording. This verse is one such promise.

Sixteen simple words are presented to us without embellishment or fanfare—a simple sentence that presents a revolutionary truth. Unfortunately, our familiarity with such statements sometimes leads us to undervalue them. Let's carefully consider these words.

Imagine if the richest person in the country came to your home and said, "I'd like you to become part of my family and be an heir to my estate. During your lifetime, I will provide for every one of your needs. From this day forward, you no longer have to worry about anything. I have sufficient wealth to take care of you."

Most of us would be thrilled beyond description to be given such a promise. We would want to tell all our friends about this incredible act of generosity. It would be foremost in our minds and we would reflect constantly on our good fortune. It would change our entire outlook on life.

In essence, this is what God has done for us. Actually, He has done much more than simply provide physical wealth. Colossians tells us that we have so much more in Christ, through whom "all things were created" (1:16) and "in whom are hidden all the treasures of wisdom and knowledge" (2:3).

Consider the power and resources available to us through such a relationship!

The context in which the promise in Philippians was given was a discussion of monetary needs and therefore its primary application is to our physical and fiscal requirements. God is telling us that He will take care of us and we are not to worry about our financial needs. This is a great consolation because one of our greatest concerns is whether our resources will be sufficient for our needs. As Jesus taught so clearly in Matthew 6:32, our heavenly Father knows what we need. The clarity of the promise before us leaves little doubt that God stands ready to provide for every financial need of His children.

Obviously then, the practical application of this truth depends on a clear definition of our needs. There is a saying often applied to this verse, "God will meet all your needs, not all your greeds!" For many of us in the western world, this is a significant issue. The standard of living that we have come to expect often far exceeds our actual needs. We must address this question if we are to enjoy the benefits and comfort of this great promise.

God calls us to a love relationship with Him in which we gladly surrender our hearts and wills. We do this because we trust that He loves us and seeks only our highest good. Part of the surrender that needs to take place is to give up our concept of what we "must have." God asks us to yield ourselves and our lives completely to Him, and in return He promises to take care of our every need.

> *Whatever needs you have in your life, God stands ready to satisfy them.*

It's similar to some monastic orders in which people take a vow of poverty. They surrender all their earthly goods to the monastic order, and from that point forward, the order assumes responsibility to provide for all the physical needs of that individual. A vital part of this arrangement is that the monk willingly submits to the monastic order and allows it to determine in what manner and at what level his physical needs will be satisfied.

As Christ followers, we are called to give our hearts and lives to God's loving and eternal purposes. In so doing, we turn over all of our rights—including our definitions of personal needs. A large part of what it means to put our faith in Jesus Christ for our salvation involves trusting Him to provide us with life beyond the grave. But it also involves trusting Him to determine our requirements in this life, and submitting to the ways He chooses to meet those needs.

While this promise speaks directly to our financial needs, the larger context makes it clear that God is speaking to the whole spectrum of human needs. Earlier in the chapter we are exhorted to not worry about anything in our lives. So God's promise to meet all our needs clearly extends beyond the simple matter of finances. Whatever needs you have in your life, God stands ready to satisfy them.

Consider the implications of such a

statement. The God who spoke the entire universe into existence has promised to care for your every need! He has clarified the promise by stating that He will meet those needs according to His glorious riches in Christ Jesus. It is clear that God wants us to understand that His willingness to provide for us is matched by His ability to do so.

Bring every unmet need you have to God. Place the desires of your heart before His throne and allow Him to determine what you truly need and what is best for you. Although you may initially feel fearful in doing this, you will find that God is trustworthy, and that He will overwhelm you with His goodness and generosity if only you will let Him.

Do not be anxious
about anything, but in everything,
by prayer and petition,
with thanksgiving,
present your requests to God.
And the peace of God,
which transcends all understanding,
will guard your hearts
and your minds in Christ Jesus.

(Philippians 4:6-7)

Day Eighteen

WORRY ABOUT NOTHING, PRAY ABOUT EVERYTHING

Everyone deals with anxiety to some degree. Some people encounter it only occasionally while others are plagued by fears and worries. But given the turmoil and unsettled days in which we live… and the personal challenges and traumas that each of us experience… anxiety is clearly a reality of living in the 21st century!

When you get to the root of worry, you find that it surfaces in our lives because deep down, each of us wants to control our environment and our destiny. We long to have things turn out the way we want them to. We don't want to be surprised by unexpected events that disrupt our idea of how things ought to be. In spite of the strength of these desires, we know that we cannot control the world around us. And if we are honest with ourselves, we'd have to admit that we can't even control ourselves all the time!

This inability to control our environment and the things that impact our lives most often leads to pain. When people behave in ways we don't want them to, we often end up frustrated and injured. If circumstances turn out poorly for us, we feel hurt. That pain can express itself in a spectrum of unhealthy behaviors that range from pulling into an emotional shell to becoming bitter, angry and aggressive in our dealings with others. The self-medicating behaviors we engage in are almost always designed to either escape or eliminate the pain.

There are many sources of anxiety including finances, health, relationships, and employment… just to name a few. Our worries are as varied as the circumstances of our lives. And when worry hits, we usually feel that it is justified. We don't feel that it is wrong to spend time and energy dwelling on our fears.

But God has a very different perspective. He makes it clear that He does not want His children to be filled with anxiety. He knows that it is a crippling emotional and spiritual disease.

It is interesting to note that the root of the word *worry* comes from a Middle English word meaning "to strangle," and the word *anxious* comes from a Latin word meaning "to torment." These are not very healthy states of mind!

Is it any wonder then that God commands us never to be anxious? He loves us too much to allow us to fall prey to this destructive force.

But most of us respond to this command by ignoring it. Something negative happens… or could potentially happen… and we worry. And we do so mainly because we don't understand how to keep from worrying!

Thankfully, God didn't just tell us what *not*

to do… He also gave us a pathway to escape from whatever anxiety is plaguing us.

That pathway is a simple, but powerful antidote: *Pray about everything*.

Notice that there are no exceptions to this command. There are no situations in your life in which God gives you a pass to indulge in worry. He has made it clear, no matter what you are facing, your response is to be the same: Bring Him your concerns and release your fears into His hands.

God's promise is that He will replace our anxiety with His peace.

This may not seem natural, but many things in life… which at first are uncomfortable… become easier with practice. By nature we do not find it easy to trust God, but as we learn to do so, worry will lose its stranglehold on our lives.

God's promise is that He will replace our

anxiety with His peace. And He makes a special point to let us know that His peace transcends all understanding. We believe by controlling our circumstances we will have peace. But God knows differently. He knows that *true* peace is the peace He gives... a peace that cannot be explained so easily. And He delights to give His children peace in the midst of difficulties that would destroy those left to their own strength. The peace He gives is durable and strong; it does not evaporate at the first sign of trouble.

We receive this peace by asking for it from our heavenly Father. But the wording in this passage implies that our request should be presented in a certain way. First, the word translated *petition* implies that we need to approach God with a spirit of humility. Second, we are instructed to make our requests with a spirit of gratitude.

When we are upset and worried, it is often

our tendency to become demanding and ungrateful as we approach God. While Scripture allows us to approach God's throne boldly and with confidence (Hebrews 4:16), it does not allow us to be arrogant or presumptuous. If we come to God with our fears and anxieties and ask for His help with humility and gratitude, He will gladly bestow His peace upon us.

What are you worried about today? What burdens and fears are you wrestling with? Whatever they are, God wants you to bring them to Him so He can replace them with His peace.

Remember that there are no exceptions to this command. No matter what you are facing, God is telling you to not let anxiety choke out your peace. When you find your mind anxiously dwelling on something, stop worrying and begin praying. It may seem unnatural at first, but if you follow God's directions, He'll give you the kind of peace your heart so deeply desires.

For a man's ways
are in full view of the LORD,
and He examines
all his paths.

(Proverbs 5:21)

Day Nineteen

GOD CARES SO MUCH, HE IS WATCHING EVERYTHING YOU DO

Every person on this planet has one thing in common: We are searching for meaning to our existence.

Over the years I have had the privilege of traveling to many different countries and seeing the variety of conditions in which people live. There are an incredible number of variables that impact people's lives: history, economy, climate, social system, political system, and religious environment.

But of the many conditions that characterize the way people live, the most dangerous and insidious is despair. Despair and hopelessness are deadly to the human soul. Human beings can endure almost anything when they still have hope, but, when that is taken away, even their will to live can disappear.

The most common cause of despair is a sense of meaninglessness. And if any person ever understood this truth it was Solomon.

Solomon was one of the richest and wisest men who ever lived. He could have had just about anything his heart desired because of his enormous wealth. He also had deep insight into matters too difficult for others to understand.

Most of us would imagine Solomon was the happiest and most contented man on earth. But he was not. When he wrote the book of Ecclesiastes, he began it by writing, "Meaningless! Meaningless! Utterly meaningless! Everything is meaningless." These do not sound like the words of a happy man, but rather those of a very depressed person.

Throughout the rest of the book, Solomon recounts his inability to find meaning in pleasure, entertainment, work, and wealth. The extent of his failure is reflected in the fact that the word *meaningless* occurs 35 times in Ecclesiastes.

So after applying all his wisdom to these matters, he concludes by saying: "Now all has been heard; here is the conclusion of the matter: Fear God and keep His commandments, for this is the whole duty of man. For God will bring every deed into judgment, including every hidden thing, whether it is good or evil" (Ecclesiastes 12:13-14).

At first glance it may appear that this conclusion is almost as depressing as the many statements of meaninglessness which preceded it. Everything... every deed... will come under the judgment of God?

While this may seem harsh and almost hopeless, upon further reflection, the contrast becomes clearer and hope begins to shine through. Our problem is that most of us have the tendency to see judgment only in a negative light. Just hearing the word conjures up images of cold, harsh, unfeeling assessments of our shortcomings and failures.

But there is another dimension to this term that can bring hope and joy to our hearts. Here is the powerful truth to be learned: *God's judgment brings meaning to our lives!*

There is never a moment of your life when your ways are not in full view of the Lord. God cares about you that much.

Perhaps you have never considered this, and if that's the case, take a moment to let it sink into your soul. What is one of the most effective ways to insult a person? To ignore them completely. To act as if they don't even exist. The opposite of this is to pay close attention to what a person does and then care enough to honestly evaluate him or her.

When I was 13 years old, I desperately wanted to make the varsity soccer team at my school. I was very sensitive to any mistakes I made during practice, thinking that they would ruin my chances of being selected. I remember one day in particular I felt the coach was singling me out for some kind of punishment. During our team scrimmage he would stop play repeatedly and correct me in front of the other players. I was so discouraged that I was sure I would never make the team.

Seeing how despondent I was, my coach called me over after practice. He told me I should not be discouraged by his criticisms and corrections because it meant that he felt I was worth the time. He pointed out that it was the players who were *not* receiving attention of any kind (good or bad) who should be worried. His words gave me a whole new perspective. It gave me hope that I would have a shot at making the team.

The truth that God "examines all your paths" shows how much He cares about the way you live your life. Your life is not an insignificant, random set of events; it is full of meaning and consequence. What you do, think and say each day has eternal repercussions. There is never a moment of your life when your ways are not in full view of the Lord. God cares about you that much. He places that much significance on you and your life.

So remember, child of God, your heavenly Father watches you each moment of your life. He loves you and cares for you more than you can possibly comprehend. He has invested eternal meaning into the moments of your existence and examines all your paths. You are a priority to the God of the universe. Live your life in light of this truth.

"*I* tell you the truth,
if you have faith as small
as a mustard seed,
you can say to this mountain,
'Move from here to there'
and it will move.
Nothing will be
impossible for you."

(Matthew 17:20)

Day Twenty

WITH FAITH IN GOD, NOTHING IS IMPOSSIBLE

Almost everyone comes to a point in their life when they must confront what seems to be an impossible situation.

If you live long enough, you will inevitably come to the end of your own resources and have the overwhelming feeling that you are powerless to change the circumstances you are facing. Your own strength, wisdom and knowledge will not be sufficient to confront the challenge before you. How should you respond at such defining moments?

In this passage, Jesus tells us that it is not our own abilities which will deliver us when we are facing an impossibility—it is our faith in Him.

It is a common practice for people to use the word *faith* in a generic way. You will hear people say, "Faith will get you through" or "Keep the faith," as if faith is some kind of entity or deity in and of itself. But faith means nothing apart from its object. The true power of faith lies in the strength and truth of its object, not in the strength of the faith one places in it.

I can believe something with all my heart, but if the object of my faith is false or untrustworthy, my trust in it is meaningless. For example, I can convince myself that I can defy the laws of gravity; I can believe that it is possible to float in midair. However, if I test my faith by stepping off the roof of a 20-story building, I will soon learn that the strength of my faith matters little. The corollary of this is also true: If the object is true and trustworthy, my faith does not have to be strong in order to release its power.

Jesus understood this truth and used a word picture to show how great the contrast can be. He tells us that our faith can be as small as a mustard seed and yet even with such miniscule belief, we can move an entire mountain! It is hard to imagine a greater contrast between two elements of the world we live in. How can something so tiny move something so enormous?

The power comes not from the tiny faith, but from the huge power and trustworthiness of the object of that faith. When your faith is in the One who made the mountain, you can begin to understand why it takes so little faith to move it!

Many Christians I have met lament their lack of faith. It is common to hear them say, "If only I had more faith!" But Jesus makes it clear to us that if we have even a minute amount of faith, we have enough to face any situation, even one which seems impossible. Perhaps an illustration will help us understand how this works.

Imagine you come to a lake in early winter and it is covered in ice. You want to walk out onto the ice, but are unsure as to whether it can bear your weight. You could proceed boldly out onto the ice with full confidence that it will support you and find yourself in freezing cold water! Or you could proceed with fear and trembling, moving slowly out onto the ice, full of doubts, and find that you are as safe as if you were on solid rock. Even if your faith was small, halting and uncertain, the strength of the object is what delivers the result.

The all-powerful God of the universe is telling you that if you trust Him even in a weak and imperfect way, He will unleash His power to do impossible things in your life.

The problem many Christians have is that we are unwilling to step out onto the ice until we feel our faith is strong enough. Somehow we have gotten the idea that we cannot move out in faith unless that faith is near perfect.

While it is important to strengthen and

deepen our faith, we often fail to understand how powerful even our weak faith can be. Many times we seem to believe that we should have no reservations, fears or doubts and that if we do have them, they completely nullify our faith. The result is a kind of paralysis in which we take no action, but instead wait for the perfect balance of trust to arrive. And it rarely does.

Take time to consider the impact of this truth in your life. Jesus often says things to us that are staggering in their implications. The all-powerful God of the universe is telling us that if we even trust Him in a weak and imperfect way, He will unleash His power to do impossible things in our lives. He goes even further by saying that if we have even tiny faith, nothing will be impossible to us. That means that we can apply our faith to every situation in our lives, even (and especially) the impossible ones.

Do not let either the familiarity or

extremeness of this promise cause it to lose its power. Reflect on what your life would look like if you began to take this promise seriously and live out its implications. Like the boy who brought Jesus his few loaves and fish, bring your small faith to Jesus and trust Him to do something extraordinary with it. Remind yourself that it is His power, and not your faith, that moves the mountains.

*H*e who did not spare
His own Son,
but gave Him up
for us all—how will He not also,
along with Him,
graciously give us all things?

(Romans 8:32)

Day Twenty One

GOD WILL GIVE YOU EVERYTHING YOU NEED THROUGH HIS SON

One of the great hindrances to growth and progress in our Christian life is that we become so familiar with statements of revolutionary truth that we end up undervaluing them. The idea of God willingly sacrificing His own Son is one of those truths.

Most of us have heard John 3:16 so often we tend to shrug at its astounding implications. But read it again, "For God so loved the world that He gave His one and only Son, that whoever believes in Him shall not perish but have eternal life."

While this verse is often quoted evangelistically, it is most extraordinary because it tells us the very nature of God's love—a love that would lead Him to sacrifice His own Son for us!

I have only one child and my daughter is the light of my life. I adore her. My love for her is deeper than any words can express. I would literally do anything or give anything to prevent her from being harmed in any way.

So what would induce me to willingly allow her to be tortured and sacrificed? Absolutely nothing! Even the hypothetical thought of voluntarily allowing her to be hurt fills me with revulsion and horror. I would literally give up everything I have, including my own life, in order to keep her safe. Those who are parents understand these feelings.

But let's say I was willing to sacrifice my daughter for you. If I was, I would only be willing to do so for one reason: Because I love you with the same depth and passion that I love her. There would be no greater expression of my love for you than that single act.

And if I were to allow such a sacrifice, you could be assured that I would give you anything else you needed. After all, I had already proved how much I love you having given up something that was most precious to me.

It's that kind of love that this verse presents us with. It's expressed in the revolutionary statement that God Himself "did not spare His own Son, but gave Him up for us all." God did what I could never do with my daughter, because God loves in a way I could never love. I hope you will pause for a moment and think about what it means to be loved so greatly!

Most of us have little trouble believing that God the Father loves His Son Jesus with an eternal love. And if He indeed loves Jesus with that kind of love, then He must love us as much if He willingly sacrificed Jesus for you and me!

Yet there are times when we struggle to feel

God's love for us. When our circumstances become difficult, it's easy for us to question whether God really loves us. We can wonder whether He is willing to answer our prayers and give us good things.

But the Bible reminds us over and over again that we can rely on God's love for us because He has already expressed the full extent of His love through the sacrifice of His Son on our behalf. Certainly, there could be no deeper expression of His love than that! Everything else pales in comparison.

God acted in human history to show His eternal love for you through the sacrifice of His Son.

So when you are having difficulty believing the reality and depth of God's love for you, consider the crucifixion of Jesus Christ. Remember that God acted decisively to prove His love for you… He did not restrict Himself to abstract statements.

You can be assured that His love is real, because genuine love always results in actions that seek the highest good of its object. And God acted in human history to show His eternal love for you through the sacrifice of His Son. It was an indelible statement of the unfathomable depth of God's love for you and me… and all mankind.

If you truly grasp this kind of love, it is impossible for your life and heart to remain unchanged as you will begin to see the implications for your life. For example, this verse tells us that God spared no expense in expressing His love for us. The logic is powerful. If God willingly gave that which was most precious to Him, then He will gladly give us everything else in His power.

The term "all things" is far-reaching in its implications. Is there anything God will not give those He loves? Only those things which He knows will *not* be good for us. Everything else in

God's storehouse is available to His children. And notice the way God promises to give us His gifts—graciously.

God wants you to live your life in the light of His love. So today, meditate on the greatness of His love for you as expressed in the sacrifice of His Son. Consider His willingness to give you everything else in His power to bless you and fill your life with good things. Claim your inheritance as His child, and boldly seek from Him everything your heart desires.

But remember this—the wrong
desires that come into your life
aren't anything new and different.
Many others have faced exactly the same
problems before you.
And no temptation is irresistible.
You can trust God to keep the
temptation from becoming so strong that
you can't stand up against it, for He has
promised this and will do what He says.
He will show you how to escape
temptation's power so that you can bear
up patiently against it.

(1 Corinthians 10:13 LB)

Day Twenty Two

EVERY TEMPTATION YOU FACE CAN BE RESISTED

Everyone who chooses to follow Christ will face temptations, even though some people think that when you give your life to God, He will take away all your problems and temptations.

Actually, the opposite is true. When you choose to trust Christ as your Savior and follow Him as your Master, you change sides in a great spiritual battle. Satan's hatred for God leads him to hate God's children... and that means you. He knows how dearly God loves you and therefore does everything in his power to separate you from God. This means that a decision to follow Christ makes you an enemy of Satan... and all his dark spiritual forces.

Temptation is one of the most powerful weapons the devil uses against you and me. Jesus

Himself was tempted by Satan, and in Matthew 4:3 the devil is referred to as "the tempter."

Another reason temptation often seems stronger for Christians is that our relationship with God gives us greater sensitivity of conscience. For those who do not follow Christ, many attitudes and practices seem harmless, even enjoyable. But with Christ dwelling in our hearts, we are more aware of things that are harmful to our souls and displeasing to God.

This is not the same as legalism, which creates a system of rules and regulations that we must obey in order to make us acceptable to God. Legalism is motivated by fear and based on guilt. A love relationship with God heightens our desire to please Him. The very fact that all our sins have been forgiven and our condemnation has been removed motivates us to obey and serve Him, and we do so without fear.

But temptation is very real and poses a challenge on several levels. The most obvious is dealing with the temptation itself. It seems that each of us has particular areas of vulnerability. What is a great source of enticement for one person may hold no attraction to another. That is why it is important to guard against pride when discussing sources of temptation.

Whatever your area of weakness, there is usually a great struggle to overcome it. And since temptation comes to us in various forms and at various times, a large part of our struggle is the need to stay alert and on guard.

Another aspect of dealing with temptation is the confusion and guilt that often surrounds it. Many times when we feel the desire to do something we know is wrong, we believe that the desire itself is sinful. Having the desire to sin is not wrong; it is a natural part of the world in which we live.

It is only when we act on our desires that they become sinful.

James 1:15 tells us, "after desire has conceived, it gives birth to sin; and sin, when it is full-grown, gives birth to death." Satan uses this confusion to discourage us. Often as we wrestle with wrong thoughts and desires, we believe we are already sinning, which lowers our resistance, leading us to succumb to the temptation.

As a predator seeks to isolate its prey from the herd, Satan whispers in our ear that no one else has such evil desires and that surely our case is hopeless.

Finally, we often struggle with a sense of isolation when we are tempted. In addition to the other difficulties we encounter, we experience even greater pressure by telling ourselves that we must be the only person in the world who has such terrible desires. This is one of Satan's most powerful tools for weakening and destroying us. As a predator seeks to isolate its prey from the herd, he whispers in our ear that no one else has such evil desires and that surely our case is hopeless. This leads us to be unwilling to share our struggles with others. The isolation we feel deprives us from gaining the strength that comes from knowing that we are not alone, and that others have been victorious over this same temptation.

These verses from 1 Corinthians speak to each level of your struggle. Be encouraged today with whatever you are struggling with as God wants you to know that, "many others have faced exactly the same problems before you." You are by no means alone in your temptation! Quite the contrary, there is nothing new or different about the wrong desires you are facing.

Not only that, the struggle you face can be overcome. God says with absolute clarity: "No temptation is irresistible." He goes on to promise that He will show you how to escape temptation's power. And the "wrong desires that come into your life" are not sins; they are temptations to sin.

One final thought for you to consider. In the Bible, there are two famous instances of temptation: the temptation of Eve in the Garden of Eden and the temptation of Jesus in the desert. In both cases Satan quotes God, but in a way that distorts the meaning of what God really said. Be assured that Satan does the same thing with you. He tries to get you to believe a distorted version of God's word. So when you are being tempted, pay careful attention to your thoughts. Be aware that Satan wants to mislead you and warp your understanding of reality. Remind yourself of what God *really* says about the temptation you are facing. That is why Jesus overcame Satan's temptation and Eve did not.

The next time you face temptation in an area of weakness, make a conscious effort to turn to God and claim His promise that He will show you a way to escape. If it helps, speak out loud to God and to Satan. James 4:7 states clearly, "Resist the devil, and he will flee from you." Tell Satan you refuse to hear his lies and tell God that you choose to submit to Him. Whether you feel anything or not, you will be transacting serious spiritual business. Confess your helplessness to God and turn your struggle over to Him—He will never let you down.

*B*ut godliness with
contentment is great gain.
For we brought nothing into the world,
and we can take nothing out of it.
But if we have food and clothing,
we will be content with that.

(1 Timothy 6:6-8)

Day Twenty Three

YOU WILL LEAVE THIS WORLD THE SAME WAY YOU ENTERED... WITH NOTHING

Most people would agree with the old adage: "You can't take it with you." Yet people still spend untold amounts of time and energy pursuing material possessions. Why?

Perhaps it's because thinking about their mortality makes people uncomfortable and so they live their lives pursuing material things as though life will never end. Or perhaps it's because people are insecure, thinking they won't have enough, so they work hard to stockpile as much as they can. Or maybe they long for something to cling to that will make them feel better about themselves, so they convince themselves that if they pile up loads of money, everything else in their world will be all right.

This desire for permanence and security is

not inherently wrong. As Dallas Willard says, every child of God is "an unceasing spiritual being with a glorious future in God's great universe." God created you for eternity, which is why you sense in your innermost being the feeling that you deserve an existence that is good, permanent and secure. This sense of destiny is a kind of internal compass that guides us all.

Juxtaposed with this profound longing for permanence and security is the undeniable brevity of life on earth. No wonder Romans 8:20 says, "For the creation was subjected to frustration."

As people strive desperately to create something solid and permanent, they know that no matter what they create, it will ultimately pass out of their control. The verses above from 1 Timothy remind us that our sense of possessing things is nothing more than a parenthesis in eternity. We brought nothing into this world and we will take nothing out of it.

One of the clear implications is that we really don't own any material goods; at best we borrow them for a time. We are only temporary residents and will someday give up all we own.

The truth of this has really struck me as I write these words in an airport in Asia. I have just traveled from the island of Saipan, where FEBC has an international transmitting site. Part of the purpose of my trip was to assist in our negotiations with the government for a land lease because our current 25-year contract is about to expire.

If you were to visit the broadcasting site FEBC has in this location, you would get an impression of permanence. There is beautiful landscaping, a number of well-constructed buildings and three massive antenna systems on the property. But the impression of permanence is not real. When we built the facility we knew that we could use the land for 25 years–beyond that, we had no guarantees. You see, on Saipan, only those born on the island are allowed to own property. Those born elsewhere can only lease land.

> The temporal and physical things we have will be of no value in the spiritual and eternal world that God promises.

This is a great picture of our life here on earth. None of us are permitted to truly own anything. As our Scripture today reminds us, we will take nothing out of this life. And nothing is an all-inclusive word! Your health, your spouse, your children, your skills, your home, your car, your money—all of them are simply "on lease" to you. And the One who grants you that lease has the right to revoke any of those "possessions" at any time. And ultimately, you will have to surrender everything when you leave this earth.

I heard the story of a father who each year

would take his children to the local landfill and tell them that everything they would ever buy or own would someday end up there. Take some time to look around you at all the stuff you have and imagine it ending up buried beneath a pile of garbage. It is not a pretty picture, but it drives home the reality of how temporal and fleeting our possessions really are.

And when you think about it, it's no big deal because the temporal and physical things we have will be of no value in the spiritual and eternal world that God promises. We won't take anything out of this life because we won't need it! In fact, the temporal nature of our possessions only serves to remind us of all we have to look forward to when we pass from this life... the permanent and eternal joy God promises us.

So we can hold our possessions loosely. And someday it will actually be a joy to release the stuff of our earthly existence when it is time for us to pass from this life to our true life.

I encourage you today to let this truth sink in. Let it set you free from the pointless pursuit of seeking your joy and security in gaining more possessions. Learn the joy of being content with what you have, and the freedom that comes from letting go of your need to possess. Practice the joy of giving freely and sacrificially of what God has entrusted to you. For as you do, your present life on earth will more closely parallel the eternal life that God has prepared for you.

I can do everything
through Him
who gives me strength.

(Philippians 4:13)

Day Twenty Four

GOD PROMISES YOU HIS STRENGTH TO FACE ANYTHING IN LIFE

This is one of the most familiar and beloved verses in the Bible… and for good reason. Everyone faces tough patches in life, and we all need the strength to face those situations. No matter how a person's life looks from the outside, you can be assured there is something they are struggling with. Dealing with pain and disappointment is just part of the human condition.

When I was in seminary, a visiting missionary made a statement that impacted me deeply. She said, "In our churches there is a broken heart in every pew." Some people face troubles and difficulties that are evident for all to see. But others face internal struggles—hidden battles—that even those close to them might not be aware of.

We all struggle. And no matter what those

struggles might be, we all need strength to face them. Which makes this promise great news!

But it's even more potent because it's all-encompassing… and that's truly comforting. You will never face a situation where you can't call on God to receive His strength!

If you give yourself completely to Jesus Christ in a posture of obedience and submission, you can be assured of having all the strength you will need to face whatever life brings your way.

Now, this promise isn't just some good-luck charm for Christians. Like all of God's commands and promises, this one must be understood and applied as an expression of His intimate relationship with us as His children. So, as we consider this great promise, we need to be sure we properly understand its context and application in order for us to realize its full benefit.

First, notice that the apostle Paul says we

can do all things "through Him." The fulfillment of this promise does not come as a form of positive thinking. Rather it comes when we embrace a life of intimacy with Jesus. Throughout the Scriptures, believers are described as being in Christ and Christ is described as being in us. When we pursue this kind of intimacy with our Lord, He gladly opens His storehouses of power and blessing. As the loving father told the brother of the prodigal son, "You are always with me, and everything I have is yours" (Luke 15:31).

It is thrilling to consider having access to all of God's resources. But we must remember that God's resources are for God's purposes. He is not our servant—we are His. Our highest calling is not to fulfill our dreams, but to do God's will.

Perhaps this sounds unattractive to you. And if it does, then you do not really understand the nature of God and how He desires to bless your life.

The Bible tells us He is "able to do immeasurably more than all we could ask or imagine" (Eph. 3:20). Yes, our highest dreams are infinitely smaller than God's plans for us.

That's no surprise, when you think about it. We tend to dream about things that are temporal, while God desires to bless us with the eternal. So don't begrudge God for wanting you to do His will rather than yours!

And it is in the doing of God's will that you are promised His strength. The "all things" or "everything" that this verse refers to can only be rightly understood as those things God calls you to do. For example, it would be pure lunacy to say, "God says I can do all things through Christ, so I will jump off a building and fly." God's power is fully available only for God's purposes. If you give yourself completely to Jesus Christ in a posture of obedience and submission, you can be assured of having all the strength you will need to face whatever life brings your way.

What is God asking you to do today? Many of us know what God wants us to do, but we lack the courage to do it. Take a moment to let the Holy Spirit speak to you clearly about some situation in your life. Claim the power of this promise as you seek to obey Him. Step out in faith and do what you believe God is calling you to do. And keep looking to Jesus to give you the strength you need, because He has promised that you can literally do anything through Him.

It is only as you test God in these practical situations that you will realize the full power of this promise.

The LORD is near
to all who call on Him,
to all who call on Him
in truth.

(Psalm 145:18)

Day Twenty Five

KNOW THAT GOD IS NEAR TO YOU WHEN YOU CALL ON HIM

One of the most common frustrations I hear from Christians is that they don't feel close to God. It seems like every Christ follower feels this at some time in their life.

Years ago, I saw a sign in an office that read, "If you don't feel close to God, guess who moved?" This is more than a pithy saying ... it's accurate theology. Many of us struggle to maintain a consistent sense of closeness with God, even though we greatly desire it, because we have hearts that are "prone to wander," as John Wesley's great hymn states.

This tendency toward self-sufficiency is part of our sinful human nature, and we must learn to overcome it.

Those of us who live in the United States have a heritage that leads us to value rugged individualism. From an early age, we are taught that we should become strong and independent. Being able to handle anything that comes our way without the help of others is highly valued. And asking for help is seen as a sign of weakness, and those who admit their inability to cope by themselves are often regarded as the rejects of society.

Each day, we are bombarded with hundreds of messages like these. But these messages are destructive to our souls because they feed our natural tendencies and lead us away from closeness with God.

When you consider the power and influence of our flesh combined with a culture that is contemptuous of those who ask for help, it is little wonder that many Christians fail in their attempts to feel close to God?

As overwhelming as these obstacles may seem, God's answer to our dilemma is actually quite simple. This wonderful promise from Psalm 145 tells us that God is near to all who call on Him in truth. Now, let's not make this any more complicated than it needs to be! There are two clear and simple conditions for the fulfillment of this promise.

First, God desires to be near to you, but you have to ask Him. He is always available, and is waiting for an invitation to engage and draw near to you. If you are struggling to feel near to God, I have a simple question for you: Have you asked Him to come near? Have you invited Him to enter into your situation? My intention is not to make you feel guilty, but rather to encourage you to actively consider the thrilling prospects of regularly inviting God's active presence in your life.

The foundation of all prayer is the recognition of our helplessness before an all-powerful and loving God. This is why through the centuries, followers of Christ have addressed God on their knees. There is nothing magical about this posture. Rather, it conveys an attitude of submission to the One being addressed. To be on your knees before God is to be vulnerable and humble in His presence.

What an astonishing concept that God would allow us to address Him with a term of such intimacy and endearment!

But God also invites us to approach Him boldly. As Hebrews 4:16 says, "Let us therefore come boldly to the throne of grace, that we may obtain mercy and find grace to help in time of need" (NKJV).

As a parent, I have marveled at the absolute boldness and lack of shame that my daughter has in petitioning me. She never hesitates to ask me for what she wants. Rachel has a wonderful way of asking for my attention and my help. It usually begins with "Daddy...." As a father, that single word spoken by my child is more compelling than anything I can think of. Rachel asks me for things constantly and without any sense of embarrassment. And why shouldn't she? She needs my help, and she knows that I love her with all of my heart and want to help her. What could be more natural than that? How much more so is this true of God, who loves us perfectly?

The second condition to enjoying a close walk with God, tells us the way in which we are to call upon God, which is "in truth." The Hebrew word used here carries the concept of stability, solidity and steadfastness. The form of the word used here occurs 125 times in the Old Testament, and in most cases refers to people or things that are trustworthy and have integrity. So, not only are we to call upon God, but we are to do so with the kind of honesty just described.

Is there stability, solidity and steadfastness in the way you call upon God? Do you do it in truth? In other words, do you really want His help and are you asking in a spirit of genuine humility? Or are you simply praying because you think there is some mystical power in the activity itself?

When my daughter asks for my help, she does it "in truth." She wants my involvement in her life and welcomes it when I respond. Over the years, she has even learned that I may say no or I may give her an answer she would rather not hear. But because she knows how deeply I love her, she steadfastly and consistently "calls upon" me as her father. Romans 8:15 tells us that because God's Holy Spirit lives in us, we cry, "Abba, Father." The nearest English translation to this is "Daddy." What an astonishing concept that God would allow us to address Him with a term of such intimacy and endearment!

Call upon your heavenly Father now. Do it with your whole heart, persistently, consistently and without embarrassment. As you do, He will come near to you and give you everything you need for this day.

$\mathcal{D}$o not
let any unwholesome talk
come out of your mouths,
but only what is helpful
for building others up
according to their needs,
that it may benefit those
who listen.

(Ephesians 4:29)

Day Twenty Six

SPEAK ONLY WORDS THAT BUILD UP OTHERS

Perhaps your life is something like mine. My days are filled with words. Each day, I encounter thousands of words from the television, the newspaper, the radio, email and the internet. But of greater impact in my life are the words spoken to me by those around me and the words that I speak to them.

Words are a powerful influence in our lives. They can be a source of strength and encouragement or they can wound and destroy. Proverbs 18:21 states, "The tongue has the power of life and death, and those who love it will eat its fruit." Each of us has witnessed the ability of words to damage and sometimes even destroy a person or a relationship. But we have also seen how the right words spoken at the right time can bring healing, restoration and renewal.

I remember experiencing the power of words during my time in seminary. As is often the case with seminary students, my wife and I had very little money. With both of us working full-time and me carrying a full load of courses, we were stressed from every side. Due to our lack of money, we had a very unpleasant housing situation, living in a noisy, roach-infested apartment. And during this time there were a number of instances when fellow believers' words to us were harsh and critical. Perhaps we needed to hear some of those corrections, but during that period even constructive criticism felt like an anchor thrown to a drowning man.

But we also experienced the healing power of kind words during those seminary days. In contrast to the hurtful criticism of some, many others spoke words of encouragement. Such expressions of affirmation felt like a drink of cold water after wandering through a barren desert. I remember times when I thought I couldn't go on. I would tell myself that I was going to quit seminary, leave the ministry and resume my business career. But then God would send someone to me with uplifting words that would literally change my mind and give me new resolve to fulfill my calling.

I learned the tremendous power of words. It has been more than 15 years since I began seminary, yet I can still recall the impact of things said to me during that period of my life. In many cases, I can remember the exact words that were spoken. The feelings and emotions that accompanied both the cutting comments and the healing words are still strong.

I want to challenge you to think deeply about the impact of your words on those around you. Ephesians 4:29 gives us a formidable command: We are not to let anything come out of our mouth that is unwholesome. The Greek word for unwholesome, *sarpos*, means rotten, worthless, bad or corrupt. This same word was often used by Jesus when He spoke of the concept of good fruit and bad fruit. That's a pretty clear picture, isn't it? Good fruit is beautiful, sweet and healthy. Bad fruit is unattractive and distasteful.

Imagine that your mouth literally dispenses fruit all day long. What kind of fruit are you offering to those around you? Is it attractive and nourishing to those who receive it? Or is it bitter and harsh?

Instead of allowing worthless and even damaging words to come from our mouths, our speech should be oriented to what is good for those around us.

Criticism, gossip, impure language, expressions of anger and other forms of negativity often dominate our conversations. God makes it clear to us that He sees these things as having no value in His Kingdom. And the reason God tells you not to speak words that are unwholesome is that He loves you and the people around you, and longs for each of us to be encouraged and built up. It's not just those on the receiving end of unwholesome speech who are hurt; such words can't pass through your lips without damaging you as well.

As is often the case in Scripture, we are first told what *not* to do, and then given direction as to what we *should* do. So the apostle Paul in today's passage tells us that instead of allowing worthless and even damaging words to come from our mouths, our speech should be oriented to what is good for those around us.

This is not simply a technique; it is a worldview and a mindset. For Christ followers, our lives are not to be lived for ourselves. Jesus Christ set the example we are to follow. His entire existence on earth was to serve those around Him, which culminated in His sacrificial death which made salvation available to all humanity. As His followers, we should serve others as Jesus did, with every faculty we possess placed at His disposal for the accomplishment of His redemptive purpose.

Have you ever had a day when you wished you had spoken more? Probably not. But many of us have had days when we wished we had spoken better. Pay close attention to the words you speak and their impact on the people around you. Commit yourself to use the gift of speech to empower, encourage and uplift those God places in your path.

And God is able to make
all grace abound to you,
so that in all things at all times,
having all that you need,
you will abound
in every good work.

(2 Corinthians 9:8)

Day Twenty Seven

GOD IS ABLE TO GIVE YOU GRACE FOR EVERY SITUATION IN LIFE

Today's promise is one of those promises from the Bible that is bursting at the seams with good news. The words convey a sense of fullness to the point of overflowing.

God has the ability to make "all grace" available to us as His children.

Of course, most Christians would acknowledge that God can do anything. But in this case, this promise is not simply an academic statement about God's power. This is a passionate promise from God to us… one that has application to every situation we face. The clear implication is that God not only is able to help you in every circumstance of life, He greatly desires to.

The overpowering strength of the language

used shows that God wants to shower you with His resources so that you will have absolutely everything you need for every good work He calls you to do.

Sometimes we live our lives as if God is fabulously rich, but very stingy. Many Christians acknowledge God's power with their lips, but live their lives in a way that paints God as a heavenly miser. Consider your own life—how you speak, how you behave, how you react to your circumstances. Do you show… in each situation you face… that you have an infinite supply of grace and power from the Creator of the universe?

If you answered this question with a resounding, "Yes!" then I applaud and admire you. You don't need to read any further because you are already fully applying this promise to your life. However, if you are like me, and this question makes you feel inadequate, I invite you to read on.

Most of the Christians I have met struggle to tap into God's resources consistently. We know in our heads that God has vast and unlimited resources, but as we live out our daily lives we often think, speak and act as if we are spiritual paupers. Why is that? I would like to suggest two reasons. First, because we don't truly believe that we have access to the resources; and second, because we don't know how to get them when we need them.

As a leader at FEBC, I have access to many different resources: an office to work in, budgeted funds to spend, computer technology, phone systems and staff support. All of these resources allow me to carry out my responsibilities far more effectively than I possibly could without them. What does it take for me to access these resources? First, I must believe that I have a right to utilize them, and second, I must know specifically how to gain access to them.

Imagine that I was having difficulty

believing I had access to all these resources. I might say, "It's true that I have been told that I can lead this ministry, but it is hard for me to believe that I could ever be worthy of such a privilege. And I know I should believe it, but I am struggling to comprehend that I have all these resources at my disposal."

God is prepared to give you far more than you are prepared to ask for.

If this were the case, I would probably not access those resources and be stifled in my leadership role.

But imagine that I did overcome my doubts, and in my pocket I had a key to the front door and a key to my office, and I had the passwords to access the security, computer and phone systems. Everything I needed to enter into the purposes and privileges of fulfilling my work. But I simply did not appropriate them correctly. I didn't use them.

Even though I had all the resources I needed, I still wouldn't be successful in my role as leader of FEBC.

This scenario may seem unrealistic and absurd. But consider carefully how little it differs from our life of faith. When FEBC called me, they gave me keys and passwords and explained what they wanted me to do. By following the instructions I was given, I had full access to all the resources I needed to carry out my calling. When God called you, He gave you keys to access all of His resources and explained what He wanted you to do with them.

In John 6:29 Jesus Christ said, "The work of God is this: to believe in the One He has sent." God is calling you to believe His promise. He is prepared to give you far more than you are prepared to ask for. Begin today to trust Him in every situation you encounter. Believe with all your heart that He has an inexhaustible supply of resources to meet every need in your life. Access those resources through faith and prayer. Watch Him work in response to your loving trust and submission to Him and His purpose for your life.

*I*n fact,
everyone who wants to live
a godly life in
Christ Jesus
will be persecuted.

(2 Timothy 3:12)

Day Twenty Eight

IF YOU ARE A CHRIST FOLLOWER, YOU WILL ENCOUNTER DIFFICULTY

The gospel is Good News, but not every aspect of it agrees with our idea of good. We tend to equate "good" with words like easy, pleasant and comfortable.

Such a perspective comes from our inclination to view our circumstances in temporal terms. As a result, much of our time and energy is spent trying to get our life here on earth comfortable and manageable. To us, the good life is a life where we have everything organized the way we like it and under control.

Many well-meaning Christians focus on living their lives in such a way that they will have peace, harmony and order. They believe that if they can achieve this, they will experience rest in their souls. Much of the behavior associated with this mindset involves isolation from the world. It ultimately means eliminating as much risk as possible and avoiding situations that may be upsetting, thereby ensuring a life of peace.

There is no question that this kind of life appeals to everyone, whether they follow Christ or not. I freely admit that if I could organize my life according to my terms, it would involve a quiet cabin in the mountains and a sailboat on a lake… my idea of a peaceful existence! But I have found that following Christ has taken me to a very different place. I have to deal with the stresses of leading a large organization, traveling around the world, leaving my family for long periods of time— none of which I would naturally choose for myself.

God's concept of the good life is radically different from ours. It comes from a view of life that is comprehensive and eternal. And in God's economy, the very things I would not have chosen have become the greatest sources of growth and blessing in my life.

Today's verse speaks to this matter very clearly. If you call yourself a follower of Christ, you can expect difficulty, and a lot of it. I love Eugene Peterson's rendering of this verse in *The Message*: "Anyone who wants to live all out for Christ is in for a lot of trouble; there's no getting around it." It can't be stated much more clearly than that!

You might be thinking that this doesn't sound very encouraging. What about all of the great promises in the Bible that we will have strength, peace, joy and victory? It's a good question. The answer is that those promises are still there, and they are still true. But victory rarely comes without some kind of struggle. As a matter of fact, *the greatness of the endeavor and victory is always in proportion to the obstacles to be overcome*. God's plan for us is not masochistic; it is realistic. We are being introduced to the realities associated with following Jesus Christ.

If you want to be a soldier, there are realities you must accept. You may receive benefits, recognition, honor and self-respect. But you also will have to endure rigorous discipline, training that is often painful, and the real possibility of physical danger, even death. A person who wants to be a professional athlete must also face all the implications of his choice. There is the prospect for great financial reward, fame, and the thrill of competition and victory. But self-denial, physical training, and serious injuries are often part of such a pursuit.

While God does not cause the problems, difficulties, and evils that enter our lives, He allows them to be the means for our spiritual growth.

I have been privileged to know many missionaries and to see the impact of their choice to follow God's call. Many experience the joy and contentment of being part of God's global purposes. But most pay a great price for their choice. The price comes in many different forms, but almost every missionary I have ever met has encountered tremendous difficulty in their lives.

The fundamental truth of today's passage is this: If you are committed to seriously following Jesus Christ as the Master of your life, you are going to encounter serious problems.

Why is this? Part of the answer is that every deep commitment carries a price tag. But there is more to it than that. I believe there are two primary reasons why this verse reflects reality for Christ followers.

First, our choice to follow Christ immediately places us in the thick of a cosmic battle. Choosing Christ as our Savior and Lord also means choosing an enemy and entering a conflict. The second reason is that God loves us too much to leave us as we are. While God does not cause the problems, difficulties, and evils that enter our lives, He allows them to be the means for our spiritual growth.

Remember, the greatness of the endeavor and victory is always in proportion to the obstacles to be overcome. As you encounter difficulties, take comfort in the knowledge that you have chosen the greatest adventure available to mankind—the pursuit of a loving relationship with the Creator of the universe. Accept all the joys and the trials that come with such a worthy and eternal journey. Learn to embrace the challenges God allows to come your way, because you know that your loving Father in heaven will ultimately use them for your good and His glory.

*I*f we confess our sins,
He is faithful and just and will forgive
us our sins and purify us from all
unrighteousness.

(1 John 1:9)

Day Twenty Nine

WHEN YOU CONFESS YOUR SINS, YOU ARE COMPLETELY CLEANSED

It has been my privilege to meet Christians from many different backgrounds and traditions. And one of the things I have observed is that a common characteristic of Christ followers is their awareness of sin. They tend to be very attuned to their own shortcomings and the areas in their lives which are not pleasing to God.

This makes sense, because by definition Christians are people who have admitted their sinfulness, know they need forgiveness, and have found the solution to both in the sacrificial death of Jesus Christ. Obviously, a person must be aware of their sinful state before they can receive the gift of salvation. This is why it is often said that the gospel must be bad news before it can truly become the Good News that it is.

However, it seems that many Christians struggle to get beyond the bad news (of their sinfulness) and fully embrace the good news (of their cleansing and forgiveness). Why? Here is one possibility.

When people first encounter the wonderful news that they are loved by God and that He wants to completely forgive their sin and give them eternal life, people are usually focused on their past sins and their future in heaven with God. However, once they enter into a personal relationship with Christ, they come in contact with the reality that many of their old sinful and rebellious behaviors persist. This can be difficult to reconcile with the concept of being completely forgiven, and the result often can be confusion and guilt.

Where does this confusion and guilt originate? Well, you can know it's not God, as 1 Corinthians 14:33 states, "God is not the author of confusion"(KJV). Whenever a particular way of thinking leads to guilt and confusion, you can be sure it does not come from God.

That leads to only one other option… Satan. There's no doubt that the devil wants to convince us of our guilt and make us question the reality and completeness of our forgiveness in Christ. He wants to throw a cloud of doubt and confusion over God's clear statements regarding this vital truth. This is the tactic he has used since the creation of the world, when he asked Eve, "Did God really say, 'You must not eat from any tree in the garden?'" (Gen. 3:1).

Today's verse from 1 John cuts through the confusion and guilt that often clouds our minds. God's statement to us on this subject is clear and unambiguous. The promise is simple: If we confess our sins, God will forgive us and cleanse us from ***all unrighteousness***.

Is there any sin that would not be covered in

such a promise? No! Does the promise say that if we repeat the same sins, they will not be forgiven? No! Do we have to do anything more than simply confess our transgressions in order to receive forgiveness? No! Must we perform some kind of penance to prove our sincerity? No!

Since the condition of this promise is that we simply confess our sins, it might be very helpful to be very clear about what this means. The Greek word for "confess" is *homologeo*, a compound form of two Greek words: *homo* meaning "the same" and *logos* meaning "word." Quite simply, biblical confession means that when we look at our sin, we "speak the same words" as God does. It means we agree with Him in recognizing that our behavior is displeasing to God and damaging to us. It may seem simple,

> *Unresolved guilt is not only emotionally unhealthy, it interferes with our ability to freely receive and enjoy the flow of God's grace into our lives.*

but it needs to be sincere. God knows whether deep in our hearts we really agree with Him or not. And when we truly agree with Him about our sin, He cleanses us of all of it—no exceptions!

The area I live in has what is known as hard water piped into our homes. It is called hard water because it contains minerals, typically calcium and magnesium. As a result, every few weeks, I notice a diminished flow of water coming from my showerhead. This is usually caused by a buildup of the minerals in the pipe. In order to correct the situation, I unscrew the showerhead and take a cloth to clean out the end of the pipe. It is a very simple process, but it must be done regularly to ensure a normal flow of water.

Because many Christ followers focus so much attention on their sin, they often let guilt build up in their lives. Unresolved guilt is not only emotionally unhealthy, it interferes with our ability to freely receive and enjoy the flow of God's grace into our lives. Clearing our hearts and minds from guilt is a simple process, but it must be done regularly through confession. Having confessed your sins, the key is to believe that God has truly cleansed you from *all* unrighteousness. Be on your guard, because it is at this point that Satan wants to make you question the reality and fullness of your cleansing.

There is tremendous power and freedom that comes when you fully believe this promise and practice it regularly. Take God at His word, and freely confess your sins to Him. Then you can freely receive His abundant grace and mercy, and experience the joy of being totally cleansed.

Then Jesus came to them
and said, "All authority in heaven
and on earth has been given to Me.
Therefore go and make disciples
of all nations, baptizing them in the name
of the Father and of the Son
and of the Holy Spirit,
and teaching them to obey everything
I have commanded you.
And surely I am with you always,
to the very end of the age."

(Matthew 28:18-20)

Day Thirty

THERE IS NO GREATER CALL OR MORE FULFILLING PURPOSE THAN TO REACH THE WHOLE WORLD WITH THE GOOD NEWS OF JESUS CHRIST

Following Christ involves many exchanges.

We give up our sinful nature for His righteousness. We allow Jesus to take our place in receiving the punishment for our sins. We trade a future of separation from God for eternal life with Him. And we give up our own self-centered agenda in exchange for God's eternal purposes.

Before knowing Christ, our lives were focused on ourselves. We spent our time and energy seeking to make ourselves comfortable and happy. Our thoughts centered on our needs and we cared little for the needs of others. In fact, Ephesians 2:3 says that before knowing Christ, all of us were "gratifying the cravings of our sinful nature and following its desires and thoughts."

But now, we have a new purpose and direction for our lives. Rather than being the master of our own lives, we now exist to know, love and serve our King.

In the passage above, Jesus shares His agenda... and His priority... with His followers. What is striking here is the scope and comprehensive nature of Jesus' words:

- Jesus has *total* authority

- He wants us to reach *all* nations

- We are to teach *everything* He has commanded us

- He is with us *always*

This extraordinary statement could only be made by God Himself. No human being could lay claim to such power, nor give such an audacious command. The command itself is staggering: We are to tell all nations everything Christ has commanded us. How could such a mission be possible?

Imagine how amazing this must have sounded to the original audience. According to Matthew 28:16, these words were spoken to the eleven remaining disciples. These men had witnessed Jesus' arrest and crucifixion. They had seen the movement of those following Him come apart at the seams.

But then Jesus appeared to them, risen from the dead. This was their proof that He was God and it was their only hope of ever fulfilling this Great Commission. They accepted the evidence, obeyed the command, and hundreds of millions throughout history have come to know Jesus Christ as their Savior and Lord.

Jesus stands before you today and gives you the same command. Does this make you feel inadequate, unprepared and overwhelmed? Good! It should, because you do not possess the resources to accomplish such a task. This command is not about you and your abilities; it's about God and His power. Perhaps that's why Jesus sandwiched the command between two amazing statements about Himself.

First, He informed His disciples that He possesses "all authority in heaven and earth." People often use the term "absolute power." In truth, no such thing exists on earth. Only Jesus Christ has absolute power, and He wanted to make sure His disciples understood this… to reassure them. He alone has all the resources needed to accomplish the task of making disciples of all nations.

Exchange your temporal and self-absorbed agenda for God's global and eternal purposes.

Aren't you glad that God's call for you to participate in His global purposes is based upon His power and not yours? As is so often the case, God's truth sets us free to rest in His power and provision for us. He would never command His children to do something without giving them everything they needed to accomplish it.

Second, Jesus promised the disciples that He would be with them always. What words of comfort! This was not a cold-hearted master giving instructions to His servants and then leaving them to fend for themselves. These are the gentle words of a loving parent, one who cares deeply about reassuring His children. A child can hear no more comforting words from his father than, "I'm right here and I'll stay with you." Whatever the challenges or fears a child might face, there is no greater way to be filled with hope or courage than to have the strong and loving reassurance of a father's presence.

What agenda dominates your time, energy and attention? Is it your personal fulfillment, your dreams, your desires? I guarantee that your plans will always be far inferior to God's. Exchange your temporal and self-absorbed agenda for God's global and eternal purposes. As you participate in God's redemptive plan to reach all nations, your horizons will be broadened, your vision will be enlarged, and your heart will be touched.

And as you engage with God's plan for the world, you will experience the absolute authority and rule of Jesus as well as His abiding presence. There is nothing more valuable or worthy in which you could invest your life. You have one life to live. Spend it well. Pour it out in obedience to God's redemptive plan.

*N*o, in all these things
we are more than conquerors
through Him who loved us.

(Romans 8:37)

Day Thirty One

NO MATTER WHAT SITUATION YOU MAY FACE, YOU ARE MORE THAN A CONQUEROR

Much of life is like walking into the middle of a movie when the hero is being besieged by his enemies. At such a time, things tend to look very grim for the good guy.

The scriptwriter often enhances the drama by making it look as if there is no possibility for victory. The enemies are so strong and the hero is so weak or so badly wounded that there seems to be no possibility he will be able to overcome them. But this is only the middle of the story!

If you stick with it and wait until the end, you will see the hero come back from a position of almost certain defeat. Miraculously, he regains his strength and completely destroys his enemies.

Do such stories strike you as foolish romanticism? Wishful thinking? They shouldn't, because I believe such ideas are branded into our consciousness by God Himself. Stories of certain defeat being turned into decisive victory appeal to us because something within us tells us that this is how things are *supposed* to be. Right should triumph over wrong.

This is why the apostle Paul wrote, "We know that the whole creation has been groaning as in the pains of childbirth right up to the present time" (Romans 8:22). Whether they follow Christ or not, everyone knows that things are not right.

As I said before, our experience on this earth is much like entering a story at its midpoint. If you do not recognize that the story is unfinished, you may be led to despair. Imagine how the disciples felt as Jesus hung on the cross.

Here was the One they had put their hopes in and had given their lives to. They had witnessed His character and His power with their own eyes.

They had seen Him heal people, turn water into wine, calm the seas and even raise the dead! How could it be possible that One with such power could be defeated by mere men with swords, ropes, nails and a cross? How could He allow Himself to be tortured and mocked? The pain and disappointment the disciples experienced at that moment must have been beyond comprehension.

How ridiculous it would have sounded at that point if an angel appeared and proclaimed, "This is Jesus the conqueror. He has overcome all the powers of evil and darkness and has forever secured the victory of His followers." It might have sounded preposterous, but it would have been true! We understand this because we know the rest of the story. We know that Jesus was victorious and that He completely crushed His opponents. We possess the knowledge that one day every knee will bow before Him and every tongue will confess that He is Lord.

This is why it is so crucial to maintain an eternal perspective. When we only look at part of the picture, we cannot correctly assess or respond to the situation we find ourselves in today. Throughout the New Testament, we are instructed and reminded about what we really are. The exercise of our faith requires that we look at the whole story and embrace what the Bible says about us as God's children.

Jesus Christ has completely conquered the powers of darkness, and thus we engage in our temporal battles with full confidence that we cannot lose!

This passage is one of those great statements about who we are because of what Jesus has done. We are called "more than conquerors." Beyond that, Paul tells us that we bear this glorious title "in all these things."

What is Paul referring to? Just two verses earlier in this passage he writes, "Who shall separate us from the love of Christ? Shall trouble or hardship or persecution or famine or nakedness or danger or sword?" The clear answer is that nothing can separate us from the love of Jesus, and that beyond that, in all of our trials, persecutions and problems, we are victorious through Him. In short, we are overcomers in every circumstance of life.

A conqueror is someone who goes through a battle or contest and emerges victorious. But what does it mean to be *more* than a conqueror? There are two elements of our spiritual struggle that qualify us for this title:

Our victory is already assured. Most people enter a conflict uncertain of the outcome. They hope to win, but cannot be assured. We, however, already know the outcome of our struggles. Jesus Christ has completely conquered the powers of darkness, and thus we engage in our temporal battles with full confidence that we cannot lose!

We can only gain from our struggles. The

Scriptures clearly teach that God takes everything in our lives and uses it for our benefit. This applies to our spiritual struggles, our trials, and the difficulties and weaknesses we experience. Even when we feel that we are losing, we are assured that God is working for our growth and benefit.

As you "fight the good fight of the faith," remind yourself that you are already more than a conqueror through Jesus Christ. Your work is to believe what God has revealed to you and to act accordingly. He has already won the victory for you! He empowers you to participate in the battle now so you will one day have a share in the glorious future He has prepared for His children.

THE AUTHOR

Gregg Harris has served in a variety of ministry positions over his career, including as a pastor at Saddleback Church under the leadership of Rick Warren. Today, Gregg serves as the president of FEBC, a non-denominational Christian radio network based in La Mirada, California.

Founded in 1945, FEBC is an international Christian radio network that broadcasts the Good News in more than 150 languages from 126 transmitters located throughout the world.

Gregg's passion is to see the truth of God's Word proclaimed to transform lives for eternity. Through FEBC, he leads a team that uses the powerful, yet personal, medium of radio to help men, women, and children come into a real, vibrant relationship with their Creator.

Gregg and his wife Betsy live in Southern California with their daughter, Rachel.

[For more information about the work of FEBC, please visit febc.org.]